After Freedom

After Freedom

*How Boomers Pursued Freedom, Questioned
Virtue, and Still Search for Meaning*

MARY VANDERGOOT

CASCADE *Books* · Eugene, Oregon

AFTER FREEDOM
How Boomers Pursued Freedom, Questioned Virtue, and Still Search for Meaning

Cascade Books
An Imprint of Wipf and Stock Publishers
199 W. 8th Ave., Suite 3
Eugene, OR 97401

www.wipfandstock.com

ISBN 13: 978-1-62032-198-0

Cataloguing-in-Publication data:

VanderGoot, Mary.

After Freedom : How Boomers Pursued Freedom, Questioned Virtue, and Still Search for Meaning / Mary VanderGoot.

x + 170 pp. ; 23 cm. Includes bibliographical references.

ISBN 13: 978-1-62032-198-0

1. Baby boom generation—United States. 2. Baby boom generation—Social aspects—United States. I. Title.

HN58 V1 2012

Manufactured in the U.S.A.

Cover image by Vandergoot Ezban Studio, used with permission.

For Two Andrews
Andrew Petter and Andrew Bender
My Father and My Grandson
They have taught me about the saga of the generations.

For everything there is a season,
And a time for every purpose under heaven.

—ECCLESIASTES 3
PETE SEEGER AND THE BYRDS

Contents

Acknowledgments · ix

PART ONE: Baby Boomer Dilemma—How Did We Get So
Socially Alienated and Spiritually Lonely?

1   The Stories · 3

2   Boomer Legacy · 15

3   Forever Young · 29

4   Liberty to License · 39

5   Is Freedom an Illusion? · 48

6   Free Opinions · 58

7   Tangled in Freedom · 66

PART TWO: Rethinking Freedom, Reclaiming Virtue,
and Searching for Meaning

8   Daring to Face the Truth About Ourselves · 79

9   Gratitude Makes a Difference · 90

10 Offloading Anger · 102

11 Recovering Attachments · 116

12 Seasoned by Care · 128

13 Reclaiming the Sacred Circle · 137

14 A Last Chapter · 151

Bibliography · 161

Acknowledgments

O N THE DAY WHEN I first sketched out a plan for this book I could not have imagined how many sources of inspiration I would discover along the way. Friends and acquaintances cheered me on by including an interesting link in emails or drawing my attention to something they had seen in the news. Some acquaintances I barely knew shared Boomer nostalgia with me once they discovered it was a topic I was researching. And my good friends asked often enough, but not too often, how my writing was coming along.

Friends in "The Writing Group" have read my essays (and sometimes my poetry) and offered feedback with keen pens and kind hearts. They understand the solitary labor of writing, but they also know how the process creates an energy all its own. Their willingness to share the adventure with me has been a great source of companionship. So to Edi, Barbara, Sylvia, Jane, Katy, Kristy, Carol, Otto, Heather, and Duane my sincerest thanks.

For several years I have been meeting regularly to read international fiction with a book club that has no official name. It is a circle of strong women, world travelers, seasoned professors, avid readers, and intellectuals with sterling credentials. What I treasure most about them is that over time they have become very good friends who offer me the sanctuary of a warm space in which to think about life and muse about what it means to grow older. Maryann, Barbara, Christiana, Johanna, Sally, and Helen represent for me a circle in which truth surfaces. For the gift of their company I am deeply grateful.

The Sunday morning Adult Education Hour at Forest Hills Presbyterian Church has offered me a lively place to think about and discuss "big questions." It is a place where the questions matter as much as the answers, and where the need to ask the same questions many times over is honored. Those who have shared those golden hours with me know who they are, but probably they vastly underestimate how much their shared interest has inspired me. To each and every one of them I express my genuine appreciation.

To the readers who agreed to preview my work in various stages and offered me their honest comments and useful advice, my sincerest thanks. Luiza Ezban, Marianna Scholte, and Richard Plantinga read the manuscript in its earliest stages and offered me helpful advice by being candid about what did and did not speak to them. Others have read the manuscript as it grew, and still others have been helpful by reading it in bits and pieces. It takes a village to write a book, and the responsibility for choosing what actually goes on the pages sometimes seems weighty, but the encouragement of others has lightened that chore. Thank you so much.

To my parents who are no longer present as they once were, but who will always be present in my heart, I express my respect. To my children Sara and Dan, Jana and Mike, who have taught me a great deal about the limits of my own generation, and who shore up my hope for a future beyond the time I can imagine, I give my blessing. And finally to Henry who has been tireless in his encouragement for this project, who has discussed many of the ideas with me many times over, and who always manages to keep clear the difference between his ideas and mine, I can only begin to express how deeply grateful I am.

PART ONE

Baby Boomer Dilemmas

*How Did We Get So Socially Alienated
and Spiritually Lonely?*

1

The Stories

> I navigate life using stories where I find them,
> and hold tight to the ones that tell me new kinds of truth.

> —BARBARA KINGSOLVER[1]

WE HAVE ALREADY PASSED the fortieth anniversary of that time in the 1960s during which young people, on the threshold of adulthood, took a stand against the mainstream culture and turned it in a new direction. Then we looked forward to what we thought we could make of our lives. Now we are in the very different position of looking back to see what came of it all.

In the 1990s, when we judged the progress of the Boomer generation by the achievements it could claim, it appeared that the quest for freedom had been successful. There was at least some progress toward enlightened social goals, the inventions of technology had blossomed into a booming economy, and the end of the Cold War had reduced the risk of nuclear disaster. Or so we thought.

By the first decade of the new millennium, however, a shadow was cast over the optimism of the 1990s. Hard on the heels of a time of great confidence we have entered a time of uncertainty. The world is confronted with the prospect of terrorism. We worry about the security of our government buildings, our food and water systems, and our mass transportation

---

1. Kingsolver, *Small Wonder*, 6.

systems. Anxiety about the irrationality of nations with nuclear arms has resurfaced.

Along with these fears about what could happen, we have actual worries arising from what has happened already. An unstable stock market and shrinking pensions, rising unemployment rates, real estate foreclosures, and huge national debt cause worry about whether our future is secure. One war after another and the tragedy of those whose lives will be permanently altered by them make us wonder if we will ever have peace again.

What we once believed could only happen elsewhere is happening to us now, and we live with a daily feeling that something has to change. *Time* magazine ran a special report on the impact a changing economy has had on regular Americans; they are people like our neighbors, relatives, and friends. They are people like us. The article read: "Sometimes we change because we want to: lose weight, go vegan, find God, get sober. But sometimes we change because we have no choice, and since this violates our manifest destiny to do as we please, it may take a while before we notice that those are often the changes we need to make most."[2]

It is easy for us to point a finger at others and claim that things would be better if they had made better choices. When after his retirement Alan Greenspan appeared before a congressional hearing he was asked if he regretted decisions he made as Chairman of the Federal Reserve. It is true he had a lot of power, and if we need someone to blame for a distressed economy, people in positions like his are good candidates.[3] Seeing our own part in the turbulence of the economy is more difficult. We do not know what we personally did to cause the problems, but we are left to cope with them.

It is hard for us to accept ownership of many problems we now face. It may be difficult for me to see the impact of climate change when I look out the windows of my own house, but it is stunning to think that my energy consumption combined with everyone else's may thin polar ice caps, alter the ecosystem of oceans, and change the prospects of survival for humans and other living things all over the globe.

In the 1950s Rachel Carson warned about trash being dumped in oceans and pesticides soaking our land, but we tended to see those as localized problems caused by others. We felt worried, but we did not feel personally responsible. We were not as prone to guilt and anxiety at that

2. Gibbs, "Special Report: Thrift Nation," 22.
3. Greenspan, *The Age of Turbulence* and "I Was Wrong!"

time. Today concerns about global warming and carbon emissions are part of our public vocabulary, and no one is excluded from collective responsibility. We are all consumers; we all contribute to the problems.[4] Do we understand the extent of our responsibility as clearly as we feel the limits of our control? Many of us are trying, but we are confused.

The beliefs that took shape in the Boomer generation were not entirely new, but they gained greater influence as they took popular forms. Central to the belief set of the Boomer generation is the ideal of freedom. Boomers sanctioned diverse lifestyles and asserted we should be able to do what we want and say what we think. The most outspoken activists of the Boomer generation were determined to level the playing field and undo notions of privilege that allowed only some to have opportunities not available to everyone. As their ideas caught on greater numbers of earnest citizens also became more sensitive to matters of injustice. In its simplest form this means that they learned to object to intrusions on individual freedom.

Even as we became preoccupied with freedom, we often continued to ignore personal responsibility, and we attended even less to collective responsibility. Boomers were uneasy with the notion that others could hold us responsible for doing right. What I do is my business. Because we thought everyone should have the same freedom from responsibility, we also became less certain we could count on others. And that raises a challenge. If I could make a difference for the better but choose not to, what does that say about my choice? Some of us would say it is our right to do what we want because we do not have to answer to others for the choices we make. Others would say that the passive course is far from benign because sins of omission, like sins of commission, must be weighed against moral responsibility, not against our freedom.

Boomers resent challenges to our accountability because we want to believe that in addition to being free we are also good. Give us freedom, and we will do what's right. We have mixed feelings about blaming ourselves for events over which we have no control, and we think it is antisocial to underestimate the good intentions of free people doing the best they can. At the same time we are unable to say much about what is right because we are convinced that each individual is entitled to have opinions about what is right and wrong. The opinions are relative. At least that is what we say, although when it comes to living this out, we do not appear to really believe it. When it comes to events that have an impact on us personally we are

4. Carson, *The Sea Around Us* and *The Silent Spring*.

quick to judge and quick to blame. Nonetheless, confusion about freedom makes it extremely difficult to talk together about "right action."

Barack Obama in his 2009 inaugural address called ours a "new era of responsibility." But how do we balance our individual freedoms and our collective commitments? How do we sustain a perception of ourselves as individuals whose choices matter while at the same time we are participants in a global culture so extensive that the significance of our individual actions is invisible?

The confident individualism by which we once defined ourselves is no longer adequate. Something about the way we are living is not working well. For nearly forty years social habits and a shared public language have bombarded us with messages about who we are. Boomers thought their vision would be carried forward into the future, but as we grow older it is becoming obvious that generations coming after us are charting their own course. In many cases they are critical of us; in some cases we are also critical of them.

Generation X, the Millennials, and the i-generation will shape the life of their own time. The full impact of where they are headed is not yet clear. They are in full bud, but not yet in full bloom. Their future is still emerging. For now Boomer culture is still a dominant force, and that means that its strengths have been expressed and its limits are being exposed. We are discovering its quandaries, and we are being challenged to face its problems.

BASICS OF BABY BOOMER CULTURE

Forty years ago when Boomers entered adulthood they built a dream around the rights of each autonomous individual to be self-determined, frank with opinions, and independent. Nothing was worse than being a conformist: no fate worse than being stifled. The pressures of tidy social patterns that controlled generations before did not fit the new agenda for freedom, and many Boomers rebelled. Some of the acting-out was intentionally outrageous, but there was much more that, although subtle, also carried forward the agenda of self-centered individualism.[5]

It is not the case that free individuals refuse to care about anyone else, nor is it true that autonomous persons lack empathy or kind hearts. *Self-centered* is not the equivalent of *selfish*. Americans deeply persuaded by a vision of personal autonomy and individual rights have accomplished

5. Gitlin, *The Sixties*.

6

many remarkable things for the benefit of their neighbors. But when we refer to Boomer culture we are not describing the private intentions of particular individuals. Rather we are voicing the common assumptions that float around in the public language of our culture, and these assumptions do center on the primary importance of the self.

The unquestioned beliefs articulated for us in media, in schools and universities, in government, and in popular literature have formed how we understand ourselves, as a society, as a group, and as a nation. We hear these claims as if they represent the way everyone else thinks, even if at times they do not describe the way we think ourselves. The views woven through the structures of our shared culture constitute an *outer* message, and to understand it we must distinguish it from our personal and private views.

As a generation we came to believe that when individual interests come into conflict with relational concerns the balance should tip in the direction of self-interest. Some would go so far as to suggest that self-interest is the propellant toward progress. In a culture committed to individual freedom words such as "duty," "obligation," or "responsibility" have negative connotations. There is a shadow of authoritarianism, old-fashioned rigidity, and top down oppression that hovers over these terms.

We would affirm someone who says, "I have decided to find new ways to participate in my community." We would be less likely to nod in agreement with someone who says, "I think I ought to fulfill my public duty." The actions might be the same, but the implication of obligation and external expectations in one case and the suggestion of voluntary participation and positive self-expression in the other make all the difference. In the mindset of public America duty crowds out freedom, and that is not acceptable because freedom is sacred. Appealing to freedom has the power that once characterized appeals to the will of the divine. Doing something because we are free to do it sounds so much better than doing something because we must.

Now after forty years of Boomer culture we may still consider freedom to be an individual right, but we are beginning to have doubts that choosing the good is something we can each do alone. Is it really an individual choice to throw motor oil down the storm drain? Is it really the private business of food handlers to decide if they want to wash their hands after bathroom breaks and before returning to work? Is it really Nadya Suleman's own business if she chooses to have octuplets in addition to six children she already has? Should adults be free to smoke in their own cars if there are children riding with them who are then compelled to breathe second-hand smoke?

In the 1960s Baby Boomers reacted against a culture that was boxed in by conformity. In *The Lonely Crowd*, David Riesman criticized Americans of the Greatest Generation for being too concerned with fitting in and too eager for the approval of others. He suggested that the demands for conformity made it impossible for persons to know each other authentically, with the result that life in a society bound up with expectations left them lonely and empty. He called them "outer-directed."[6]

Around the same time Richard Yates portrayed the mentality of the 50s in his novel, *Revolutionary Road*. It is the basis for the film by the same title directed by Sam Mendes and released in 2010. When interviewed about the message of his novel Yates says: "I think I meant it more as an indictment of American life in the 1950s. Because during the Fifties there was a general lust for conformity all over this country, by no means only in the suburbs—a kind of blind, desperate clinging to safety and security at any price."[7]

As a new generation of Boomers broke out of the lonely crowd, they formed *youth culture*. During the 1960s this term had a meaning independent of age. It embodied the intention to be *forever young* or forever new by not giving in to tradition and the past. It is the embodiment of modernity: turning away from the past and setting sights on the future. Many who were taken up in the energy of youth culture sincerely believed that they were creating a new society in which the present would be valued over the past, revolution would counter conformity, and youth would challenge authority. In other words, progress would be continuous. The vision was captured in the slogan: "Today is the first day of the rest of your life."[8]

Although Baby Boomers did break through the constraints of conformity, we did not overcome the burden of loneliness. The freedom we pursued made our sense of community uncertain. Now forty years later we are facing problems that require discipline, cooperation, and commitment. Threats to world peace, the challenge of preserving the environment, concerns about global health, and the intricacies of a world economy are

6. Riesman, *The Lonely Crowd*.

7. Clark and Henry, "An Interview with Richard Yates."

8. The words "forever young" were used by Bob Dylan as a song title. "Today is the first day of the rest of your life" is often credited to Abbie Hoffman. Both were used so widely in youth culture that the sources are unclear.

not purely individual matters. We are realizing that we need more than freedom and the autonomous choices of individuals to deal with them.

There are social critics who speak up from time to time to suggest that the Boomers and those who are following after them cannot solve current problems because they are indifferent, self-indulgent, and lazy. In addition to being insulting this explanation is unproductive. It does not recognize that solving our problems requires more than action. Instead we need help redefining who we are, clarifying the principles by which we are determined to live, and doing that together.

What if after working hard to establish our individual freedoms we are now confused about what it would mean to join together to embrace solutions? Perhaps we cannot see how we could go about doing that without forfeiting the freedoms we have committed ourselves to and that we are so willing to rise up to defend. We are not lazy. We are caught in a quandary that batters us with contradictions. We have become tangled up in our freedoms.

This is the dilemma of the Boomer generation. We cast our lot with freedom and discovered that freedom is not enough. Meanwhile we do not see how we can move forward from a radically individual understanding of our freedom to a deeper and broader sense of freedom that can sustain our ability to live well together in a shared world. What basis do we have for joining with each other? We deserve better than a stampede of fear or a return to old habits of conformity, but on what deeper foundation can we base cooperation?

If free ways of thinking are so compulsively free that they insulate us from each other and block progress toward cooperation, we need to re-think them. If comfortable habits of freethinking rhetoric undermine our communities and accentuate our separateness so that we become isolated and powerless, we may need to tolerate the discomfort and uncertainty that come with questioning them. However, that being said, questioning freedom is tantamount to sacrilege in many places.

WHY PERSONAL STORIES MATTER

Where do we begin? The most fruitful device for clarifying how we understand ourselves is the process of telling stories. The stories of the Boomer generation are two kinds. The first are stories about culture, the culture of the United States since the 1960s. These stories recount a history of changes experienced by a group of 70 million people. They provide an assemblage of meanings reflected in language and revealed in the events that are identified as having marked the timeline of a generation. These are not stories about who I am or who you are; they are stories about who *we* are.

A second set of stories recounts the personal lives of Baby Boomers, the two decades of their childhood and the four decades of their adulthood. The cultural reflections and the individual stories are not entirely separate because they are narratives drawn from many of the same events. But they do have different perspectives.

Individual narratives resonate with cultural stories in many ways, but personal stories are far more specific because they are about someone with a name, a family, and relationships within a group of persons whose lives intersect each other. The owner of the story has some control over the course of events the story traces. When I tell my own story it becomes clear to me that I did not get to choose much of what shaped the Boomer generation, but I have been able to choose many things that charted the course of my personal life. My story recounts what I did, and at least to some degree it is fair to say that I made my story. I chose my destiny.

I do not have this same sense of agency or choice when I tell the story of my generation. When I describe what a generation thought, said, or did, I am often dipping into what has been aptly described by the psychologist Jerome Bruner as "folk psychology." He writes: "An obvious premise of our folk psychology, for example, is that people have beliefs and desires: we *believe* that the world is organized in certain ways, that we *want* certain things, that some things *matter* more than others, and so on."[9]

Before I go further with this discussion I owe my reader an honest statement about my interest in personal stories. I am a psychotherapist and have spent roughly thirty thousand hours in private conversations with clients. In the therapeutic space clients step out of the flurry of daily life and into a space conducive to dialogue. The therapist listens, and clients unfold their stories. A story or parts of it may be told many times over, altered as necessary, amended to reflect current decisions, enlarged with new insights, until gradually the narrative begins to fall together into a pattern that makes sense. Having a personal story, not a perfect story but an understandable one, is very important to most people. It is a base on which their identity is built.

---

9. Bruner, *Acts of Meaning*, 39.

The conversations of therapy use the language of mass culture and they refer to significant events that form a generation. In addition the conversations of therapy are personal. Consider the complexity of the question being asked by someone who says, "Why did I do that?" *That* may mean move to Kansas, rob a bank, marry someone, get addicted to heroin, or buy a lottery ticket that won. Each of these could change a life significantly.

In response to the invitation to speak and the assurance that I will listen, my clients tell me about important people and events in their lives. We talk about the same events that interest philosophers, sociologists, artists, medical professionals, entertainers, economists, religious teachers, political leaders, and anyone else who is trying to make sense of life. My clients tell me about things they discuss with their friends, read in books of popular culture, and encounter in films, stories, and music. And they tell me what happened to them yesterday. They search for *personal meaning* reflected to them from all these sources.

The matters my clients explore with me are intentionally subjective and personally important. A psychotherapeutic approach to uncovering truth does not by its nature have a claim to being better than any other approach we may take in addressing our concerns about truth, but the therapeutic approach does have the advantage of immediacy. It works close to the places in real people's lives where they make their decisions, experience the consequences of those decisions, and then are challenged to discover that by choosing their own actions they are agents of their own destiny.

Telling the story is a search for meaning. What clients do in therapy is similar to what we all do as we sort through the events of our own lives. Stories mirror for us who we are. They reflect who we want to be. We want to live well. We are eager for meaning. We want to live so that the present will not be empty, and so that we will not have regret in the future. Most of us are concerned both to uncover what is true and to discern what is good. We develop maps for the inner evaluations that allow us to judge if who we are is who we feel we should be.

Some of us assemble our stories more deliberately than others, but every one of us is a storyteller in some sense. That is what it means that we are conscious of ourselves. In telling and retelling our stories the narratives change because we are learning through telling. Sometimes we see ourselves in new ways because we ask questions we have never asked before. We surprise ourselves. Sometimes we discover things about ourselves that are difficult to admit. At times the telling is stressful and laborious, but at other times it is great relief. We seem most driven to tell our stories when the old ones are fracturing. In the face of quandaries our stories beg to be told.

The story that we tell about ourselves is about our past, but it is also about our future. The form the story takes begins to reveal not only how we understand what has shaped us up until now, but also what we think we are becoming. It does not end abruptly with the present as if we are accounting only for events that are already on record as having happened and about which we can give some objective accounting. The philosopher Charles Taylor suggests that the telling of my story reveals "the shape of my life *as a whole*," some of which is future. Furthermore he suggests that the questions or concerns I raise about myself "touch on the nature of the good that I orient myself by and on the way I am placed in relation to it."

Taylor uses an interesting metaphor to aid him in expressing the importance of our considerations about identity. He says that we "exist in a space of questions." The way we answer those questions defines who we are. It gives us our basic orientation. About this space he says: "We want our lives to have meaning, or weight, or substance, or to grow towards some fullness. . . . But this means our *whole* lives. If necessary we want the future to 'redeem' the past, to make it part of a life story which has a sense of purpose, to take it up in a meaningful unity."[10]

What is further significant about the space of questions is that it is a shared space. The very telling of a story requires language. It is a language that we share with others. And the accounts woven into our story involve other people and events we experience together. It is not our story alone. The philosopher Alasdair MacIntyre uses a literary metaphor to describe the self as both an author and an actor. Part of the story is made for us and part of it we make ourselves. He writes in his book, *After Virtue*, that the self (whom he calls the agent) is both an author and an actor. He suggests we are co-authors: "We enter upon a stage which we did not design and we find ourselves part of an action that was not of our making. Each of us being a main character in his own drama plays subordinate parts in the dramas of others, and each drama constrains the others."[11]

10. Taylor, *Sources of the Self*, 50–51.
11. MacIntyre, *After Virtue*, 198–99.

THE TENSION BETWEEN PERSONAL STORIES
AND CULTURAL STORIES

As we explore our individual stories the self-understanding we assemble becomes increasingly distinct from our culture's view of persons in general. That there are two stories does not set individuals over against culture. We are part of culture, and culture is part of us. Still there is a mismatch between the two stories, and we live in the tension of that inconsistency. When we view ourselves from within a personal story, seasoned by honest reflection, we come to a different sense about *the truth of what we know*, and we come to different conclusions about *the nature of our freedom*. In telling our personal story we move through and beyond our cultural story.

We keep trying to figure out what we can trust to be true. We want to know that we can live good and meaningful lives. We want something trustworthy on which to base our decisions, and we long for some source of certainty from which we can venture out and to which we can return as we navigate life. Even if we do not find answers to all of our questions, at least we seem pushed to live with the questions more consciously.

By expanding our awareness beyond the perimeter of self-interest, we increase our consciousness that we live in a shared world. The stories of our personal lives give testimony to the fact that our choices and our actions make a difference for us and for others. Many things we once thought were important seem less so now. The things we still find important are often more important than ever. Time writes our story.

We have changed, but we also return to the same questions that face every generation. What does it mean to be human? What does it mean that not just anyone but *I, in particular*, have lived? What does it mean that the short while each of us lives is book-ended by birth and death? What is the value of life? What is the significance of the fact that we live with others? Why is there suffering? Do our choices make any difference in the long run? We continue to search for meaning.

Reflecting on the search for meaning in the Baby Boomer generation is the project of this book. Part One reviews our cultural story. In particular it examines how the bold pursuit of dogmatic freedom unseated the foundations of our sense of meaning. Cultural transformation over the past forty years has tangled up our collective views of freedom, truth, and power. Rather than being exhilarated by our freedom we have become anxious and cynical.

Part Two explores the meaning of our individual choices. What we do matters to others, and what others do matters to us. We may no longer trust that answers to life's big questions will be delivered to us ready-made, but despite the pervasive skepticism of the Boomer era, the way we construct our personal stories has everything to do with whether the meaning of our lives deepens or whether the haunts of meaninglessness increasingly overtake us. Can we release ourselves from the entanglements into which our detachment from the past and our pursuit of freedom have driven us?

2

Boomer Legacy

The first forty years of life give us the text;
the next thirty supply the commentary on it.

—ARTHUR SCHOPENHAUER[1]

BABY BOOMERS ARE THE generation born after the Second World War. They are the children of the Greatest Generation. The era of the Boomers introduced color television, the moonwalk, birth control pills, computers, cell phones, and microwaves. These significant developments are symbols of American ingenuity, but standing by themselves they do not reveal the heart and soul of the Boomer generation.

The last forty years have been a time of unimaginable progress and at the same time an era of deep cynicism that cut to the taproot of our convictions. The most popular writers include the most negative. The most powerful leaders have been some of the most undisciplined, and some of the most successful financiers have been the least ethical. Each generation engages the search for meaning in its own way, but in the Boomer generation this has been intensified by the fact that our deepest convictions are in flux, and we are anxious. We are a generation that changed our habits, and we changed our minds. The results of that are not what we imagined.

1. Schopenhauer, *Counsels and Maxims*, 1599.

THE CHILDREN OF THE GREATEST GENERATION

The parents of the Baby Boomers reached young adulthood during the Second World War. As a group they were as sure of themselves and their values as any before and since in the generations that mark the identity of Americans since 1776.[2] They knew for what they stood and were willing to put their lives on the line in the Second World War because they believed they were going to war for the future of the United States, their country. They were survivors.

The down to earth, hard-working pragmatists of the Greatest Generation were unshakeable in their faith in progress, but there was nothing magical about the progress in which they believed. They were convinced that progress followed from determination and hard work. They had faith in the future, and they tended to agree for the most part with Henry Ford who had said way back in 1916 that "History is more or less bunk. It's tradition. We don't want tradition. We want to live in the present, and the only history that is worth a tinker's damn is the history we make today."[3]

While we may think of the Greatest Generation as solid traditionalists, in fact they were not. They also had lived through an era in which they broke with the past represented by their parents. Their break with confidence in tradition reached ordinary citizens both in Europe and in the United States after the First World War during which twenty million people died while the privileged of Europe quarreled over their rights and the borders of their empires. The conflict accomplished nothing for the ordinary people who suffered most for it. War left demolished villages and fields strewn with rotting corpses. Men returned from battle missing their limbs or their eyesight; many were cruelly scarred by exploding munitions or the frostbite they suffered during savage winters in the trenches. All across Europe there were towns and villages missing a whole generation of men, those who had died in the war.

When I was a very little girl I had a very old uncle who was a World War I veteran. Before he visited us the adults warned the children that we were to be very cautious about slamming doors or making loud noises. My uncle had spent long months in the trenches in France until in one bombardment he ended up with a badly broken body and shrapnel in his

2. Referring to the citizens of the United States as Americans is nearly unavoidable, but referring to the United States as America may be avoided out of respect for the other nations of the hemisphere.

3. De Coster, "Henry Ford."

back. He was evacuated to a hospital in Britain where his bones were set and his back healed, and eventually he returned to his parents and the quiet family farm in Northern Michigan. My uncle was a hard worker and a smart farmer, and by all appearances he had a good life. But he never recovered from what in quiet voices was explained to us children as *shell shock*. Unexpected loud noises triggered his panic attacks. Today we would say he suffered from post-traumatic stress disorder (PTSD). That is what he brought home with him from World War I.

The great irony of the First World War was the depth of despair felt by those who won it. When American soldiers came home from war with stories of what they had witnessed, and when their communities came to terms with the loss of those who never returned, they had to admit how little had been achieved by this gruesome venture. For whose sake had it been fought? It became clear to many that fighting a war to defend the rights of the privileged was not a sacrifice they would be willing to make again. They determined to be the guardians of their own future.

Trust in authority changed after the First World War. The government, the university, the church, and the leaders of civil society would never again be able to count on unquestioned loyalty. Leaders would have to prove themselves. They would have to give clear evidence that they too were part of the great American Dream that was intended for everyone, not just for the powerful and privileged. What previously had been an obligation to conform to authority now became an option that depended on a leader's ability to establish credibility and trust. In short there was a great democratizing of society, at least on the level of ideals. This was the atmosphere in which the Greatest Generation was raised.

The First World War was followed by the economic shocks of the Great Depression and soon after that by the Second World War, but that was a different sort of war in the perception of the American people. It began in the Pacific with an attack against the United States in Pearl Harbor. And it began in Europe with a threat to our Allies. Once again Americans went to war, but this time fighting Americans believed it was a war to preserve their own country and their own freedoms. It was a stand against threatening empires in Germany and Japan. The efforts of those who went to war were backed at home by an enormous surge of patriotism and sacrifice.[4]

When soldiers came home from the Second World War they were greeted as heroes. They had proved themselves. Citizens at home who had

4. Westbrook, *Why We Fought.*

sacrificed their domestic tranquility by sending spouses and children into war believed they had interrupted their lives for a cause that was honorable. The women who worked in factories to produce what was needed by the military felt they too had been part of the victory. Ordinary citizens who had lived on rations believed they had made sacrifices for the common good. It was a very patriotic time.

After the war, young men who had never dreamed of going to college went to school on the GI bill.[5] Women who might otherwise never have dreamed of going to work were feeling confident about themselves and the jobs into which they had stepped to replace the men who had gone off to war. Americans were feeling strong, brave, and optimistic. They were ready to settle down, to have their own little house and family, and to get back to work in the march of progress. They started having babies, lots of them. Thus the *baby boom* for which a generation is named.

This is the story of the Boomers' parents. Measured by standards of loyalty, courage, and determination many of them were simple heroes. They chose as their own heroes ordinary people who accomplished extraordinary things. They admired Wilbur and Orville Wright who proved that humans could fly; Alexander Graham Bell who found a way to send his voice over a wire; and Alexander Fleming, whose discovery of penicillin reduced the dread of common diseases. These were heroes the Greatest Generation could understand.

THE CHILDREN OF MASS CULTURE

The Baby-Boomers absorbed their parents' optimism, and they were raised on their parents' models of independence. Stories in children's books honored self-made men (and a few women): Carnegie, Rockefeller, and Astor who had started with nothing and made something of themselves. Classrooms had images of the building of the railroad to the west coast of the United States, the Brooklyn Bridge, Charles Lindbergh in his airplane, and researchers in white lab coats discovering miracles in test tubes. School children were encouraged to learn math so that their country could win in the race to conquer space.

Little boys and girls in American cities and suburbs donned cowboy hats and fringed jackets like the heroes they saw on TV. These men who were at home on the range were also fearless and self-sufficient. They lived in

5. Department of Veterans Affairs, "Born of Controversy: The GI Bill of Rights."

simple circumstances and could defend themselves if necessary. They were iconic Americans.[6]

The major league baseball player was also a hero, as much admired as the President of the United States. Boys courted fantasies of the team they would play for someday. The baseball dream was enticing because if you gave the boy a mitt, a ball, and a bat, he could begin to practice with the neighbor kids out on a vacant lot or in the street in front of their homes. That was the way Babe Ruth, Ty Cobb, and Joe DiMaggio had done it. They were not aristocrats, but they were heroes.[7]

In the early 1950s the United States was in flux. The nation was experiencing a post-war flood of immigrants from many different countries. African Americans were also becoming a more visible group in urban centers as they moved from the rural south to the industrial cities of the north.[8] Young soldiers returning from the Second World War married and set up households, and this resulted in a great surge of growth in the economy. It was a time of economic hope for many Americans.

The United States has always been a vast mix of people, and this variety has contributed significantly to its vitality. Although there has never been a standard American in actuality, there has usually been an image that the wide diversity of Americans believed represented "the real" American. From generation to generation and from era to era these ideal Americans were added to the expanding gallery of heroes: Horatio Alger, Paul Revere, Johnny Appleseed, Daniel Boone, Henry Ford, Jonas Salk, Mickey Mantle, Amelia Earhart, Frank Sinatra, and John Glenn.

For many these exemplars of the American spirit served as the definition of what an American is. In fact most Americans did not look like them, speak like them, or live like them. However, that did not detract from the admiration Americans bestowed on their cultural icons. The more you could make yourself resemble these heroic figures, the more proudly American you believed you had the right to be. The greater the difference between them and you, the less you felt like a real American.

Immigrant Americans with accents and old country habits, ethnic Americans with cherished memories about another time and place, and Americans who were visibly identifiable as members of minorities always felt

---

6. De Angelo, "The Cowboy Code."

7. Falkner, *The Last Hero*. Oakley, *Baseball's Last Golden Age*.

8. Maloney, "African American Migration to the North: New Evidence from the 1910s." Boehm, *Making a Way Out of No Way*.

they had two identities. They were Americans, grateful to live in the United States and deeply loyal to the country that adopted them, but they also had a lingering sense that they were not real Americans like all the rest. They did not resemble the icons, and they knew it.

The double identity of immigrants and minorities in the United States is a complex phenomenon. The one identity resonates with the American ideal, and the other clings to the comfort of home among the people you truly know. The one reflects what you think you should be like if you can. The other identity is the comfortable and familiar one into the safety of which you retreat because there you are accepted as you are. The one represents the prospects for progress and success, although at some risk, but the other includes those who are loyal to you even though you are slightly embarrassed by them. It is a tug-of-war in the heart.[9]

The vast majority of families in the United States lived with this double identity in some generation, because in the family tree of most Americans there is a memory of being transplanted. The process of assimilation goes through stages. Sometimes fitting in seems to matter most. At other times clinging to what remains of a sense of past is a more powerful force in the formation of personal identity. Of course the Native Peoples are the exception in the sense that they were not transplanted. They were displaced, however, and they too have gone through various stages of assimilating to the majority culture that overshadowed their own, and then, realizing their loss, returning to native ways and the heritage of their elders.

These plural selves of many Americans give rise to a phenomenon about which we are reticent to speak because right along with the streak of independence, of which Americans are so proud, there is a powerful inclination to conform. Those who wish to join the march of progress and be part of the American Dream must assimilate. This is the drama of the American Melting Pot.

THE MIRROR OF TELEVISION

In the 1950s the draw of conformity became even more powerful as Americans of all sorts looked into the mirror of television. It reflected back to them images like Ward and June Cleaver and the boys, an all American family. Alongside them were family members of *Father Knows Best* who were introduced as "your neighbors, the Andersons." These prototypes of

9. Gerstle, *American Crucible*. Miller, *Ethnic Images in American Film and Television*.

the American way lived in tidy homes, had a family car, and the dad had a job that supported the family well. He was clearly in charge while mom feathered the nest and kept the peace. Most important, the children in the families were happy, obedient, and bound for success. They embodied the promise of progress.[10]

We may wonder how many Americans actually lived the way the iconic Americans of television programs lived. Probably far fewer than we think. What we do know is that huge numbers of Americans were consumers of these images day after day and week after week. What they saw became a standard against which they measured themselves. In many instances it must have battered their self-esteem, and made them aware that they were not like everyone else. But there was always a little promise lurking behind the image. If you tried hard enough you could become a little more like the rest. And if you could not do it yourself, then perhaps your children could.

Television had been invented before the Second World War, but less than 1 percent of the households in the United States had a television in 1945. Furthermore, during the war the production of television and broadcasting equipment for civilian use was put on hold for three years while manufacturing was put to the service of the war effort. When the war ended and soldiers and sailors came flooding home at the end of the 1940s, Americans turned to domesticity and television was part of it. By 1954 over half of all households in the United States had television, and by 1962 that number had grown to over 90 percent. That was when the Baby Boomers were entering adolescence.[11]

The television set was part of the family circle. It had a prominent place in the room where the family gathered. When the family drew together around it, the TV was treated like a guest of honor. It got undivided attention and did most of the talking. It created the common vocabulary, and its shows were consumed by all members of the household regardless of their age, gender, education, economic status, or roles in the family. Television was a great equalizer in the American household.

Americans watched mothers whose bad luck was turned to good luck on *Queen for a Day*. The lucky woman was treated like royalty and sent home with advice about what laundry detergent to use, but also with

10. Marsh and Brooks, *The Complete Dictionary of Prime Time Network and Cable TV Shows 1946-Present*. Rapping, *The Looking Glass World of Nonfiction TV*. Youman and Schulman, *How Sweet It Was*.

11. Federal Communications Commission (FCC), *Golden Age of 1930s to 1950s*. Stephens, *History of Television*.

luxuries including the new appliances that every progressive American household was supposed to have on its wish list. Having this dose of the American Dream made her a queen even if only for a day.

In our neighborhood there was a girl whose mother had died. Often her grandmother was at their home taking care of the household, and my friend and her grandmother were ardent fans of *Queen for a Day*. It occurs to me now that although my friend had no mother, she was absorbing the script for the woman she was supposed to become. The television was her role model, a stand-in for her absent mother.

Americans became familiar with family men like Ward Cleaver, Andy Griffith, and Rob Petrie. They were loyal to their children, and could fix whatever went wrong. Children on television were mischievous and adventuresome, but they never got hurt beyond what could heal and never got into a fix out of which they could not get with a little help from dad. Best of all the children on television were model children who soaked up whatever their parents taught them, and were eager to follow good advice. The viewer knew beyond a doubt, these children would grow up to be good Americans. Ironically we now know that many of the child actors we saw on television found it difficult to grow up in the glow of fame that required they sustain the image of ideal children.

Regardless of how many Americans actually lived the way the Cleavers, the Andersons, or the Griffiths lived, the images were predictably there week after week until the people in the stories did seem like real neighbors. The characters merged with the actors so that they seemed to become people we knew, and sometimes the events that we witnessed on the glass screens in our own living rooms seemed truer than life. If the images on the screen did not match our own lives, we still were inclined to believe that they were a close match to how everyone else lived. And it was not something of which to be proud if we were not like them.

Behind the scenes of television was another reality that bound us even closer to the belief that what we saw on television had something to do with us. The Nielsen ratings measured what it was that people actually did watch on television.[12] Advertisers used that information to determine on which shows they should purchase time to promote their products. Television had a tight feedback loop. We thought that we watched what television offered, but actually television offered us what we preferred to watch. Feeding our preferences made more money for both broadcasters and their advertisers.

12. Nielsen Media, "Television History."

The shows about which we felt most enthused also told us by means of advertising what we needed, what we wanted, and what we deserved. It portrayed a standard against which we measured ourselves, sometimes consciously and sometimes without even realizing what we were doing. Like advice from a good friend, or at least from someone whose company we enjoyed, the ads played on our sense of value and dignity. They left us with impressions about what everyone else was like, even though we had no way of knowing if that was indeed the case. Television reminded us incessantly that we should not be left out when our neighbors were getting ahead. We should strive to keep up. Not only did we watch television, we trusted it. Television trained us to be consumers.

ALL THAT CHANGED IN THE 1960S

What we watched during the early years of television was the dream of the United States that our parents of the Greatest Generation had desired for themselves and for us. By the 1960s the dream began to come apart at the seams. As the Boomers grew up the adult culture they discovered was not one they could accept. What they had been promised seemed like an old-fashioned fairy tale that had been fiction all along. What they got was entirely different.

By the 1960s television became a source for news. There has been no more lasting and recognizable figure in the world of news than Walter Cronkite. Some of his earliest broadcasts were titled "You are There." And in Cronkite's authoritative voice the viewers were told: "What sort of day was it? A day like all days, filled with those events that alter and illuminate our times . . . and you were there."

In 1962 CBS began a nightly news broadcast, and many Americans formed their schedules around it. They had dinner early so they could watch the news, or they ate their dinners from TV trays so that they could sit in front of the television. For a half hour Walter Cronkite would tell us what had happened all over the world that day, and at the end of his broadcast just before he closed by announcing the date he would say: "And that's the way it is."[13]

Americans were confident that the news was giving them a reliable view of things happening beyond the range of what they could see

13. American Journalism Review, "*Walter Cronkite.*" Cronkite, *Eye on the World.* Kurlansky, *1968: The Year That Rocked the World.*

personally. It opened up the world to them and expanded their consciousness. Once they had seen something on the news "with their own eyes" it felt as if they had been there to witness it firsthand. They trusted those serious men who sat behind the desks of their broadcast studios and brought images of the day's events, and then told their viewers "that's the way it is."

The things Americans saw worried them. They lost hold of the comforting belief that even on days when everything was not rolling along smoothly at their own house, most Americans were still about as happy as the citizens of Mayberry, protected by their trustworthy and kind-hearted sheriff, Andy. There were too many images that did not fit that picture.

They saw their president felled by an assassin's bullet in November 1963. They saw his blood-spattered widow escort his body back to Washington. They saw his children following the funeral cortege.

Americans saw a march on Washington in August 1963. Familiar faces were there: leaders of labor, religion, and the entertainment industries joined with civil rights leaders. Two hundred fifty thousand people gathered in Washington to demonstrate peacefully. They heard Reverend Martin Luther King Jr. declare "I Have a Dream." Within a few years they saw him gunned down in Memphis.

In January 1964 they watched President Lyndon B. Johnson declare a war on poverty in his State of the Union message. It was clear that not everyone had a job, and not every family was living comfortably like the images of television.

In August 1964 the news reported the death of three civil rights workers in Mississippi. They were killed because they were registering African American voters.

Later in the fall of 1964 protests began on college campuses across the nation as young Americans spoke out against the Vietnam War. On the news Americans were confronted with images of gruesome battles, body counts, and bomb attacks. There was a military draft that could call on any young man to go into the savagery of war if his number came up. The draft and the war were real.

These are only a few of the most dramatic and highly publicized events Americans were confronted with on television. It was a tsunami of distress, and it began to shift their perception of who they were. Youth in particular suspected that the American Dream was far from the reality of their cities, their communities, and their families. If previously they had been able to push away attacks on their dream by convincing themselves that problems were only temporary or far away, that no longer seemed possible. There were huge problems everywhere. Americans were tuned in and watching.

The Boomers who were just coming through adolescence and into adulthood had two reactions to the fading American Dream. The first was a flight into the fantasies of the Flower Children. They discarded the work ethic and the discipline of their parents, and they fled to places where they could set care aside. They gathered at Woodstock where they could get stoned, listen to music, and make free love. They fled to San Francisco where they could live on the streets, share food, play music, and escape into psychedelic bliss while welcoming the Age of Aquarius: a time of love, peace, and understanding that was coming soon.

The Flower Children were fleeing from a world by which they were bitterly disappointed. In their enclaves of freedom they temporarily escaped the burdens placed upon them by the bad decisions of their parents, the government, and the organized part of society, which they called "The Establishment." Dismissing any responsibility for the ugliness they had inherited, the Flower Children also discarded any concern about tomorrow. It was a dreamy time, but it was not the American Dream that captured their attention. When Flower Children answered the call to the Summer of Love in San Francisco or similar gatherings around the country, they were advised to wear flowers in their hair, and they were promised they would meet gentle people for a love-in. It was escape into fantasy.

It was not clear what the love-in would be about. The well-known song by the Mamas and the Papas described it as a "whole new generation with a new explanation. People in motion."[14] But of one thing they were sure: they were not going to follow the example of their parents. The new generation jettisoned loyalty to The Establishment. If folks over thirty could do no better than form a world as disastrous as the one young people saw on TV, then the new generation wanted no part of it. They were going to enjoy life while they could.

The escape did not last indefinitely. By autumn 1967 there was a ceremony for the "death of the hippie" and the Summer of Love seemed to disperse as rapidly as it had formed. The utopia was recognized as a failure, and the participants returned home or wandered off to settle in places far less visible and far more isolated than the cities in which they had gathered for the Summer of Love.[15]

14. Mamas and the Papas, "If You Are Going to San Francisco."
15. Chase, "Lost in the Sixties."

In Mark Vonnegut's memoir, *Eden Express*, he tells of his life as a hippie on a commune in British Columbia.[16] They lived as much as possible from the earth, created a life in which money hardly existed, and kept as far from civilization as possible. Drugs were abundant, sex was free, and music expressed the sentiments of their utopian vision. Vonnegut's own tour through the counterculture ended with his hospitalization for drug-induced schizophrenia and his return to civilization to become a medical doctor. Not all hippies were as lucky.

Other reactions were more sober. Young radicals organized protests. They took over the office of the President of Columbia University, vandalized the campus, and closed down the school for a time.[17] In a similar fashion four hundred campuses nationwide were disrupted with protests and graffiti. University walls carried messages such as: "Make love not war!" "Nixon withdraw as your father should have!" "Stop the pigs!" "Question authority!"

On campuses where one decade before students had worn sport coats and ties now they walked around with bare feet, wore jeans, and had beads around their necks. The well-groomed military haircut of the 1950s was replaced by the uncut, unwashed hair of the hippies. Where not long before young adults aspired to the image of intellectuals smoking pipes, they now smoked pot. It was a world loaded with symbols that distinguished the present from the past.

Unrest went beyond college campuses. Protestors demonstrated in the dreadful pockets of poverty in the ghettos of large cities. Following a riot in Los Angeles in 1965 other riots broke out in Detroit, Newark, Memphis, Tampa, Milwaukee, and other large cities. Cities were burning. Store fronts and whole neighborhoods. In an effort by the police to clear the streets after dark many cities had curfews. Riots were started in prisons, and guards were held hostage. Banks were bombed, and threats were made against large corporations, those thought to have connections to the government and the war effort. A bomb was set off in the Pentagon. Demonstrators demanded "Power to the People."

Grief about the bombing of villages in Vietnam, the injury of children and noncombatants by napalm, and the loss of American lives in combat set off protest against the government. The nation was shocked when in November 1965 Norman Morrison set himself on fire under the window of

16. Vonnegut, *Eden Express*.

17. Rudd, *Underground*. da Cruz, "Columbia University 1968."

the Secretary of Defense at the Pentagon. He had gone to the Pentagon with a group of protesters, and as he marched he carried his child. Just before dousing himself with flammable fluid and striking the flame, he handed his child to a friend. Morrison was a devout Quaker who believed he was giving his life to demonstrate the misery of war and his solidarity with the suffering people of Vietnam. One week later Roger La Porte set himself on fire in front of the United Nations. The nation watched in horror.[18]

Among the most closely watched protests was the demonstration in Chicago during the Democratic Convention of 1968. The disdain of the protestors was unmistakable. They brought a pig to Chicago and demanded that it be nominated for the presidency. They screamed at the more than 25,000 uniformed law enforcement officers who had been called up for the occasion. It was broadcast live, and the nation watched.

Chanting crowds demanded, "Give peace a chance." Some shouted, "Kill the pigs!" More than 500 were arrested. Television showed images of police beating demonstrators with nightsticks, and other images of demonstrators being dragged away for arrest. At least some of the television audience wondered if this was the beginning of a revolution, another civil war. The most fearful wondered if this kind of protest could grow to a volume sufficient to topple the government. In any case it was clear that there was now a counterculture taking its stance against the dominant culture.

The nation watched as eight leaders of the Chicago protests were brought to trial. The trial was a drama, the collision of culture and counterculture played out on the stage of the courtroom. Bobby Seale raged at Judge Julius Hoffman, calling him a "fascist" and a "pig." At first the judge gagged Seale and chained him to his chair, but eventually the courtroom became so chaotic that Judge Hoffman removed Seale from the courtroom, and he was tried in a separate proceeding. The trial for the remaining seven continued. Eventually some charges were dropped, some convictions made, and a few of the Chicago Seven served time.

The rage of protest around the country subsided eventually. Cam-puses were cleaned, graffiti was sandblasted off the walls, and students returned to school. The war ended after a few more very tense years, and the draft was no longer necessary. The Vietnam veterans, whose honor was bruised by the failure of the nation to honor the sacrifices they had made, came home and tried to find their place among other young Americans. Some of the most outspoken protestors joined university faculties. The inner city

18. Hollyday, "Grace Like a Balm."

riots settled down, and some civil rights legislation was passed. Obviously all the problems were not solved, but the energy to challenge them changed. It is interesting to note what happened to the Chicago Seven:

1. John Froines became a Director of a federal agency and eventually taught at UCLA.

2. Lee Weiner went to work for the Anti-Defamation League of B'Nai B'rith.

3. Abbie Hoffman died of a drug overdose in 1989.

4. Jerry Rubin became an entrepreneur. He died in 1994.

5. Rennie Davis became a follower of Guru Maharaj Ji.

6. David Dellinger continued to be a political activist.

7. Tom Hayden served in the California State Assembly and State Senate.

Protestors of the 1960s continued to pursue change, but most of them eventually worked from within the mainstream. Those who had been branded as anti-American took responsible places in institutions and government where they explained their role in the protests of the era as their passion to call the United States back to its highest ideals. They became reformers rather than revolutionaries. In the course of their protests the Boomers had changed minds and altered the trajectory of the nation, and the hopes of the Greatest Generation had been disrupted beyond repair. The new generation of Boomers put the past behind them and determined to be young forever.

3

Forever Young

Parents are the bones on which children sharpen their teeth.

—PETER USTINOV[1]

WE CONTINUE TO LIVE in a world fascinated by the possibility of progress, but our ideas of progress have few underlying values. We share a vision of technological progress, but we do not share a vision of the future that is based in our identity as persons and our deepest convictions of what is right and wrong, what is wholesome or unhealthy, what builds us up or breaks us down morally. We have trained new experts, but they are not the experts who can shape our vision of a meaningful life. They are experts who can fix our practical problems. We place enormous power in the hands of inventors without bothering to ask if they are wise enough to merit our trust in them.

If plastic bags fill up landfills we find a chemist who can invent biodegradable ones. If as we age we make too many trips to the bathroom, a pharmaceutical company will invent a pill that will calm down the bladder. Telephones were a great convenience, but we decided that having our own number connected to a wall at home was limiting, especially if we were not there. First we invented answering machines. Then mobile phones. Now our cell phones are smart phones that keep us connected to the Internet and to social networks that span the globe. We have instant links to any

1. Ustinov, *Dear Me*, 329.

information we think we need. Streaming news keeps us up to the minute about the stock market, travel, weather, sports, or any events of importance to us. We can use them to do our shopping and our banking.

What we invented is impressive. However, our moral sense did not keep pace with our practical genius. Spiritual grounding became less and less a matter of concern in public life. While we were busy solving practical problems, we did not have much time for looking into our souls. Now and then a voice would raise questions about life's meaning and our cultural values. Christopher Lasch wrote a book about *The Culture of Narcissism*. Scott Peck wrote and sold millions of copies of *The Road Less Traveled*. We were warned about the risk of emptiness, alienation, moral disintegration, and loss of community. Nevertheless progress seemed to sweep us on past the warnings, and we cast our lot with the intention to trust progress and be forever young. That meant we would not have to look back.

As we were remodeling our world we did not consider what busy optimists are inclined to overlook. We did not consider that with each new invention that changes our world in ways that delight us, it also changes our world in ways that we ourselves do not understand until later. We never imagined that the miracles of medicine would save lives and also create economic problems as the costs of health care mushroomed. On the day that an elated public watched a moon landing in 1969 it was not thinking that the orbiting mass of high tech trash left behind in space would threaten future space travelers. Only a few decades later we must contend with the hazard this garbage poses for our global communication satellites and our cell phones.

With the discovery of plastic, which we considered a miracle material, we did not anticipate that birds on isolated islands in the middle of the Pacific Ocean would be dying from a gut full of plastic (tooth-brushes, packing material, and ball point pens) because they mistake the junk we throw into our oceans for the food they need to survive.[2] Nor when we unpacked our first home computers in the 1990s did we consider that within ten years the computer could become a tool for thieves who, sitting in front of screens a half world away, can steal our identity or hack into our bank accounts.

Can we say that we wish progress had never been made? If we could go back in time and make the decisions again, we would probably make

---

2. Lepisto, "Shocking Space Debris Images." Moltz, "Space Jam." Broad, "Orbiting Junk, Once a Nuisance, Is Now a Threat."

them the same way. It is not clear that we would be willing to sacrifice either the excitement or the convenience of our invented world. Opportunity has pushed us forward, and we have already broken out of the restraints that can hold us back. We made our commitment to the future when we accepted the ideal of being young forever.

Unfortunately progress is not enough to keep us content; we need somewhere to turn when progress disappoints us. Where is that safe place to which we can go to reorient ourselves when our dreams fade? The skepticism that mushroomed in the 1960s has continued to grow. We question authority and doubt that truth is anything more than a strong opinion. We resist the idea that *good* could be something more than one person's opinion or a passing fashion. Disoriented, because we have not been able to find a new basis for understanding our time and ourselves, we have discovered that living without firm assumptions may not be as exhilarating as we thought. Freedom can be anxious. Doubt no matter how vogue or how bold can be empty.

In an age of science and progress our questions about spiritual meaning are awkward. We understand that the absence of convenience breeds annoyance, and we think we have figured out what to do about that. We have a harder time facing the possibility that the absence of meaning creates angst. We try to adjust ourselves to living in that vacuum, because we cannot find much help in addressing it. We try five o'clock cocktails, Prozac, Jacuzzis, meditation, compulsive spending, and relaxation exercises to reduce stress, but we have not found a way to fill the meaning void. Our angst continues.

THE EROSION OF PRINCIPLE

In the era of the Greatest Generation a collection of ideas about right actions and good living allowed people to make judgments about what they believed had worth. When people gathered together around these judgments they formed community. These affiliations were not just towns or cities defined by a locality but fellowship defined by a common purpose. Such communities offered avenues into which members could direct their energies through work, family connections, friendship patterns, and institutions.

The civil rights movement, which was not tied to a place, was a fellowship of conviction. It was sustained by deep faith and a common purpose.

Martin Luther King Jr. was a hero, but not only because he was a martyr. He would also have been a hero had he lived, because he knew that his cause was righteous, and he was able to inspire others to listen to their conscience.

As we move into the twenty-first century words like *principle, fellowship,* and *hero* have become old-fashioned. Baby Boomers, Generation X, and the Millennials do not have lasting heroes because we build people up and tear them down more rapidly than ever before. The idea of principle feels too restrictive, and fellowship sounds too much like obligation. We prefer to hang loose. Short memories and shallow loyalties fit better with our lifestyles and our tastes. At the very minimum it seems that in order to be acceptable our commitments must be optional. That way we are free to change them if we encounter something we like better.

Thinking deeper than the surface of events is not a fit strategy in the information age. Not only are we aware of events instantly, we get layers of reaction and comment immediately. We often find ourselves lost in an information blizzard. Quickly the quantity of information becomes more than we can process. It deteriorates from chat to chatter which overloads us and causes information fatigue. We cease thinking actively and become passive observers. Finally, we become disinterested and move on.

The avenues through which we receive information and the channels through which we express ourselves are disconnected. We seldom have ongoing conversation with someone who hears and considers what we say, responds with respect, and sticks with us as we process our concerns to a thoughtful conclusion. How often are we able to carry on a sustained dialogue that extends over many contacts and a significant length of time? The opportunities for serious two-way conversations are rare. We often feel that we are mute in a world full of contradictory messages.

The loss of dialogue may be one of the reasons that some of the most poignant things we say appear on coffee mugs, bumper stickers, and t-shirts. We try to reduce them to unmistakably clear and evocative statements of seven words or less. Sadly we do not really know who reads our bumper stickers. When it comes to our coffee mugs, it is probably we ourselves who take most seriously what is written on them. They are a monologue we choose for ourselves. A cup of comfort.

Most Boomers grew up in an era when people did not have things written on their clothes and labels were hidden on the inside. The messages now written to be worn in public have little impact. We are accustomed to seeing human billboards, and we have learned to ignore them. Furthermore, we

32

do not know each other well enough to discuss the messages we broadcast. It would be slightly odd, if not inappropriate, to walk up to a stranger and begin discussing the bold statement on his t-shirt. He would probably be quick to tell you to mind your own business. The in-your-face statements worn in public are intentionally one-way communications.

We live on the surface of ourselves, running our lives from day-planners and to-do lists. Our contacts are cyber connections we form with people who "friend" us on social networking sites. These pseudo connections allow us to self-disclose without real intimacy. They lighten the obligations of relationships while broadening the expanse of exposure. Where is the time for deepening our knowledge of something we can trust to have enduring meaning? Even if we carve out the time, with whom can we share it?

Sherry Turkle in her book, *Alone Together*, portrays so vividly the double-binds of technology that allow us to be connected all the time and alienated nonetheless. It is touching that she chose to write about this as she was sending her daughter off to college. Practically it has never been easier to stay in touch while launching a child into a world separate from parents. It seems fair to say, however, that it has never been harder to trust the process because these children are launched into a world with so many conflicting messages and such profound uncertainty about what is worth holding onto. Sherry Turkle says it this way: "We are lonely but fearful of intimacy. . . . Our networked life allows us to hide from each other, even as we are tethered to each other.[3]

THE END OF HEROES

Abraham Lincoln was a hero of my childhood, but now I know that he suffered from desperate melancholia. I also know that he violated his own sense of justice when he let his armies march through the south, devastating towns and killing civilians. Every year produces a new batch of books about Abraham Lincoln, and with each batch he seems less a hero. A few years ago I was standing in the Lincoln Memorial in Washington DC, and nearby was a young man standing with a woman whom I assume was his mother. He was explaining to her that Abraham Lincoln was a racist at the start of the Civil War and only changed his mind for political reasons.[4] Clearly Lincoln was not this young man's hero. Who was Abraham Lincoln

3. Turkle, *Alone Together*, 1.
4. Gates, "The Root: Was Lincoln a Racist?"

anyway? Could it be that all we have left to say about him is that he was not who we thought he was?

I once thought that John F. Kennedy was a hero. He was the one who said, "Ask not what your country can do for you; ask what you can do for your country." Now I know that in his quest for power he seduced the public with images of Camelot. There are still some people who remember the Cuban Missile Crisis and the Bay of Pigs. They remember Kennedy because he let them down. We remember him as a powerful man with a beautiful wife, a president who was felled by an assassin's bullet, and a member of the family whose members have met untimely deaths. The memories of the constructive things he accomplished are rapidly fading. What happened to the hero? Was he who we thought he was?

That is the way it has gone with many of our heroes. We can admire them for a time, and then the "truth" about them comes out. We discover that they are just like everyone else, and more human than we can accept. The Beatles got older and did not get along with each other anymore even though once upon a time they sang, "all you need is love." Einstein may have been brilliant, but he was abusive of his wife and abandoned his children. Picasso was a narcissist. Van Gogh was insane. Politicians take bribes. Doctors get perks from pharmaceutical companies, and we end up taking drugs for which we pay inflated prices.[5] Where have all the heroes gone?

While we do not have lasting heroes, we do have celebrities. We briefly pay attention to winners on *American Idol* or an athlete who comes out of nowhere and captures the attention of the fans and the sports writers. Our ability to coin terms like *Linsanity* or *Tebowing* is an admission to how vaporous and temporary our infatuations are. We are caught by the hype; the persons who serve as raw material for these dramas are incidental. Street vendors print t-shirts and posters of them. They get a brief spot in the news. Then someone else takes over and nudges them out of place. Old news is boring, and rapid fluctuations in our attention do not allow us to know much about them really because they are a flash in the pan.

Some of our celebrities are antiheroes. Anna Nicole Smith's rise from exotic dancer, to billionaire's bimbo, to model in men's magazines, and then finally as a pop culture figure was tracked by paparazzi. When she died her

---

5. Gabor, *Einstein's Wife and Other Women of Genius*. Gilot, *Life with Picasso*. Now Public, "11 New Jersey Politicians Arrested." Harris, "Crackdown on Doctors Who Take Kickbacks."

image was plastered across the news. Now the drama of her life is past and we hardly remember who she was. Anna who?

Britney Spears got our attention while she was rising to fame as a sex idol for little girls who have barely reached puberty. We paid attention to her acting out: shaving her head, disrobing in front of cameras on a beach, partying at the bar dressed in a mini-skirt and not wearing underwear. Then finally we watched her tragic battle for the custody of her children because the court judged her to be an unfit mother. And now she has faded into the boring background along with all those who have been replaced by others whose drama or tragedy is more recent.

Why is there an audience for the blurry images of pop figures in a car surrounded by news hounds trying to take a picture through the windshield? Because they are entertaining? Are they interesting as examples of all the things that can go wrong for those who for a brief moment in the limelight seemed to have it all going their way? Are failures more entertaining than heroes because we do not take heroes seriously anymore?

THE DECLINE OF INSTITUTIONS

Just as our heroes have faded, similarly institutions have grown weak and out of date. In the 1950s the psychologist Abraham Maslow formulated a model of basic human needs. The most fundamental were those he called deficiency needs, and he believed that when they are unfilled it triggers angst. Maslow suggested that every healthy person has the need for belonging to a reference group, affiliation that roots a sense of identity. Belonging has two sides: access to the benefits of the group and the obligation to sustain and support it. For a long time Maslow's theory appeared in nearly every major textbook for Introductory Psychology, but now it seems old-fashioned. The idea that we owe loyalty to a group does not fit with being young forever. It interferes with our right to create our own future as we please.[6]

In recent studies of American life the highly regarded political scientist Robert Putnam has focused on what he refers to as "social capital." He means by this features of social life (networks, norms, and trust) that enable participants to act together to pursue objectives they share. In his extensive research of many aspects of social life Putnam has found that in each succeeding decade since the 1960s Americans have been less involved in

6. Maslow, "Theory of Human Motivation."

PART ONE: Baby Boomer Dilemma

community life. He includes in this such associations as discussion groups, sports clubs, PTA, labor unions, and churches. He also includes in it such informal contacts as having coffee with a friend. In his work he has made famous the idea that now more than in the past Americans are "bowling alone," and this has become a catchy metaphor for social isolation. Parallel to this decline in involvement is a decline in civic trust.[7]

When the Boomers were children we trusted that leaders knew what we didn't, and they would teach us what we needed to know. We believed our teachers; we believed them even if we did not like them. The Girl Scouts and Boy Scouts were dedicated to helping us build skill and character. Our places of worship promoted good values and moral living. And, back in those days we still had pillars of the community, those adults who represented for us what a good citizen should be.

Today we hear about predatory priests but seldom about the good ones. There is news about school superintendants who mismanage funds, but little news about those who commit their careers to educating children. We know about police chiefs whose departments are corrupt because they cover up misbehavior, but we hardly know the names of the ones who risk their lives to reduce crime and keep communities safe.

In the past institutions served as stable anchor points for persons who shared a common vision. Government, university, public schools, places of worship, non-profit community organizations, and civic leaders could line up to agree on many basic points. They did not agree about everything, but they did agree about the American Dream. They had a shared vision of the United States, its people, and its way of life. That is no longer the case.

Not long ago a Catholic friend told me that she appreciates being Catholic because it helps her to think through what is right and wrong. There are many things about the Catholic Church with which she disagrees. She questions its teachings on birth control, its procedures for marriage and annulment, and its stand on homosexuality. She values both belonging to and disagreeing with the Church because it offers her a good debate. Not always standing with it, in fact often standing against the Church helps her define herself. In this respect she is a true child of the Boomer generation.

---

7. Putnam, *Bowling Alone*.

THE LOSS OF COMMON CAUSE

Where do we find common cause? It is often where we cross paths with persons who feel critical of the same things we do. I go to a house of prayer on the occasion of a young person's rite of passage. A few days later I hear about debate in a school system that cannot decide if it is appropriate for young people in school drama programs to perform *Fiddler on the Roof* or *A Christmas Carol* because these shows are sectarian. I attend a meeting for an organization that creates safe houses for women who are victims of domestic violence. The next day I am at the movies watching a trailer in which heroes are shooting up a town and burning buildings. One of the bad guys in this film is a woman. The young fellows a few rows behind me are revved up by the spectacle. They are making degrading and sexist comments about her.

Over and over again the views that fund my choices and the beliefs that direct my actions are called into question. There is little sustained fellowship and even less community in which I can sort my authentic values. Occasionally there is an assemblage of persons who join forces for a time to accomplish some specific task. We sign petitions to get a stop light at a busy intersection. We go door to door to collect donations for a charitable cause. We help out the booster club at the local school. But these projects are temporary. They are not the kind of durable fellowship that forms our identity, a community of conviction that builds a context for addressing life's deepest concerns. Where can that be found?

What does it mean when more energy goes into tearing down than building up? We chose it that way when the ideals of youth culture became the dominant culture. When negotiation and consensus are dying arts we are caught between the moment of belief and the crush of skepticism. The potential for conflict has increased since the advent of globalism. Voices are more fractious since the expansion of militarism. The pace is faster with the capacity for instant images beamed by satellite to bring events to us electronically as they happen. Caught in the blitz of events we often feel small, and our uncertainty runs deep. We are freer now, but we are also less secure.

WHO AM I? IT DEPENDS WHEN YOU ASK ME

Without heroes, without institutions, without a sense of belonging we are at a loss for an answer when we ask, "Who am I?" The Americans of the Greatest Generation answered that question with a statement of their principles and goals. They stood behind their heroes, and accepted limits necessary for civility. They believed in hard work, progress, and a better world for their families and themselves.

We may remember with nostalgia the community concerns of an older generation. They went to church or synagogue, to the same one for years and years. They had neighbors with whom they were acquainted over a lifetime. Companies had annual picnics. Neighborhoods had parades on the Fourth of July. People kept strong connections with family and friends, and they gathered with great diligence around events that kept happening. They had a sense of belonging.

We are not like our parents who seemed so confident about their way of life. We feel entitled to believe whatever we want, but cannot decide what that should be. We have more personal freedoms than any generation before us, but we do not know what to do with our freedom. What can we believe? What does it mean to be free? We have a difficult time getting ourselves in focus.[8] So when we try to answer the question about who we are, all we can say is, "I don't know. It depends when you ask me."

8. Stephens, "To Thine Own Selves Be True." Dodson, "The Post-modern Intensification of Humanistic Psychology: A Non-lecture of Disinformation." Gergen, *The Saturated Self.*

4

Liberty to License

We feel free when we escape—
even if it be but from the frying pan into the fire.

—ERIC HOFFER[1]

Who said freedom is a picnic, and everyone's invited?

—ANONYMOUS

IN 1776 AMERICANS MADE their claim to national identity. At the birth of the country the Founders rejected privileges of birth that entitled monarchs and royalty to wield power over others. They joined together to question all political power except that delegated by the people and for the service of the people. Patrick Henry, an American hero, is still remembered for a speech he made in 1775 in which he declared: "Is life so dear, or peace so sweet as to be purchased at the price of chains and slavery . . . as for me, give me liberty or give me death." In the 1950s school children were taught the story of Patrick Henry and encouraged to believe, like Patrick Henry, that liberty is more precious than life itself. These children were Boomers.

---

1. Hoffer, "Quotes."

FREEDOM AS LIBERTY

Tragically, at the very moment of the nation's birth it was already compromising its vision of liberty. The rebels shed their own chains of oppression but did not extend the same rights of liberty to those around them who were bound by the chains of slavery. Patrick Henry made his famous speech before the House of Burgesses in Richmond, Virginia, just blocks away from the Shockoe Bottom District, which was one of the busiest slave markets in the United States.[2] Slave trade continued there for another century.

James Madison, the fourth President of the United States, fought a second war against the British in 1812. He stood up against a great military power because he was fortified by a belief in independence and freedom. The British burned Washington but could not squelch the will of Americans to be free. We also know from historical documents of the time that James Madison, the fearless patriot, kept slaves to run his household and his plantation. In his will he left instructions that at the death of his wife, Dolley, his slaves should be freed. It never happened because Dolley sold off their assets to support herself financially in her old age; those assets included their slaves.[3]

In the view of most historians James and Dolley Madison were great Americans; Dolley is one of the most revered women in the early history of the United States. Unfortunately their story also illustrates that it is easier to judge the righteousness of power wielded over us than it is to judge the power that we ourselves wield over others. Opportunities for wealth, success, or security often override the moral sense that ideals are meant to inspire.

Although we want the principles of democracy to protect us, we do not want those same principles to weaken our place in the pecking order. Particularly in times of social change we become fearful that persons like us will lose the advantage of our position relative to everyone else. As much as we may be committed to freedom, each of us also has anti-democratic instincts that are self-serving.

The 1960s was a breakthrough decade for those who believed they were being discriminated against on the basis of gender, race, or habits of life. They spoke up and demanded change. The status of women changed in the United States. After the founding of the nation women were not

2. Mack, "The History of Shockoe Bottom."
3. Allgor, *A Perfect Union: Dolley Madison and the Creation of the American Nation.*

franchised to vote for another 150 years, and even after they were able to vote they continued to be limited in owning property and transacting business. The women's liberation movement tuned the public consciousness to these sorts of inequities.

Ivy League universities, which were the guardians of reason and democracy, did not admit women until the 1960s. There was nothing subtle about the fact that the universities that claimed to educate the nation's leaders did not educate the nation's women. The first co-ed classes were Boomers. Today more than half of the Presidents in the Ivy League are women. As welcomed as that is, it is honest to remember that this was a change that took place only in the last generation.

Race relations also began to change during the 1960s. Martin Luther King Jr. was the voice of the movement. During his lifetime the FBI tracked his moves, bugged his phones, and placed observers with cameras in the large public gatherings at which King spoke. He was judged to be a dangerous person, a threat to national security. At the other extreme militant protestors charged that King compromised too much with an oppressive society. They belittled his commitment to nonviolence and accused him of cowardice. He endured criticism from all sides. Today he is an American hero, but that was not always so.

The struggle for democracy has traced its way through successive waves of immigration. Except for the Native Peoples all Americans are immigrants, but that does not seem to have softened their hearts toward newcomers. The base of the Statue of Liberty reads:

> Give me your tired, your poor,
> Your huddled masses yearning to breathe free,
> The wretched refuse of your teeming shore.
> Send these, the homeless tempest-tost to me,
> I lift my lamp beside the golden door.

Despite this honorable statement immigrants have seldom been warmly received, and the doorways through which they entered were not portals of gold. When immigrants of one generation finally assimilated enough to feel that the United States was their country, they often became the inhospitable critics of the next wave of newcomers. Once the Irish and Italians were hated. Later Eastern Europeans were belittled. United States citizens of Japanese heritage were stripped of their possessions and held in internment camps during the Second World War. The list goes on, and it is long.

Most belittled of all were the Native Peoples who were here first but are still often treated as outsiders.[4]

There is a dark streak of judgment and rejection in the history of the United States, and it lives side by side with our belief in freedom. Bigotry ends when its victims are able to take a stand and object to the way they are treated, because democracy is not a system of natural generosity. Free people seldom offer freedom to others, even though they sometimes use the rhetoric of liberty and freedom to justify their own acts of aggression. Nevertheless, at the heart of democracy is belief in the right of people to claim that to which they are entitled, and some limits to retaliation against them when they do. That is how liberty plays out.

If there has been progress in democracy, it has been achieved by successive generations who made injustice uncomfortable for their oppressors until finally withholding freedom no longer balanced out to a benefit on the side of the privileged. The legal protections of liberty allow persons to speak their minds, propound their values, and gather with others of like mind to form an identity. That is an ongoing theme in the cultural story of the United States. Democracy counts on the commitment of a majority to respond to the continuing challenges of minorities, and it counts on minorities to mount the challenges, because it is through dissent that the contradictions of our social life are exposed.

Although we have often failed to live up to our ideals, the lodestar of liberty is essential to our collective conscience. Despite the fact that we do it imperfectly, we still cling to a founding document that professes the belief that all persons "are created equal and endowed by their creator with certain inalienable rights . . ." Faith in liberty is what makes the flag important to many in the United States, a phenomenon that the citizens of other nations find difficult to comprehend.

There are few other countries in which three colors of cloth stitched together as stripes and stars could evoke such feelings of devotion. But the devotion of Americans to their flag is not to cloth; it is to freedom. The cloth stands in for the republic, and citizens pledge loyalty to that for which it stands, liberty and justice for all. In the 1960s many among the politically disillusioned refused to stand for the pledge or they remained silent while others recited it. These gestures stated their conviction that the most fundamental principles were out of balance, and they feared for the future

4. Miller, *Ethnic Images in American Film and Television*. Davis, "The Founding Immigrants."

of liberty. Among critics and defenders of the nation, the flag is an object that evokes deep sentiments about America and freedom.

FREEDOM AS PERSONAL LICENSE

Four hundred fifty thousand people gathered in 1969 at Woodstock for a music festival that was a celebration of peace and music. It was billed as "An Aquarian Explosion." Richie Havens was the opening performer. The band for which he was waiting did not arrive, and Richie just kept playing. As he was running out of songs he started to strum his guitar and sing the word *freedom*. The lyrics were simple, but the impact was powerful.

The crowd sitting on the ground listening to Richie's words knew exactly what he meant when he sang, "something's wrong." They were convinced that something had to change, and it had to move away from restraint and toward peace and freedom. In the rhetoric of youth culture the word *freedom* served many functions: a goal as in *I wanna be free*, a reason as in *I did it cuz I'm free*, or a compliment as in *he's free, man, he's really free*. In an interview nearly four decades after Woodstock, Richie Havens says: "It was the beginning of the world as far I was concerned."[5]

Who can be against Freedom? In our generation it is probably more accurate to speak of plural freedoms because there are numerous currents of freedom that became important in the 1960s. One pertained to matters of democratic and political freedom. Equally important were new freedoms that granted personal license. It is this second sense of freedom that ignited at Woodstock. Many, like Richie Havens, believed theirs was the first generation truly to embrace the possibilities of personal freedom. Not the freedom of the nation, but their own.

The claim that the world changed at Woodstock may be a little grandiose, but a profound change was taking place in the United States. The ideal of freedom which once had been defined as a collective commitment to protect each other's rights was being revised to include the freedom of individuals to have what they wanted and do as they pleased. It was not liberty protected by all for the sake of all; it was independence claimed by each in his or her own interest. It was counterculture. The Occupy Movement that has resurfaced after the first decade of the new millennium bears an interesting resemblance to the protests of the 60s.[6]

5. NPR (National Public Radio), "Havens Relives 'Freedom.'"
6. Law, "1960s Counterculture."

The freedom movement would have gone forward without Woodstock or Haven's song because young people of the 1960s were primed for change. Boomers had discovered the sins of their parents. They knew them in detail: economic exploitation, racism, sexism, corruption in government, and war. The youthful critics of their parents' generation had witnessed disregard for those who could not defend themselves, hypocritical authority, and institutional privilege.

Boomers wanted a fresh start, and they were convinced that freedom was their right, even if it meant breaking up the cultural solidarity that had meant so much to their parents. That is why some young people burned the flag or defaced it by using the fabric for shirts or underwear. They wanted to say "No!" to what the United States had become. They still linked freedom with justice because they thought the law should protect them, but they wanted more than justice for themselves. They also wanted personal license.

Youth culture had many features of adolescence, which is not surprising given that many of its participants were just stepping into adulthood. Men grew long hair and women shed their bras. Some refused to wash; they wore beads, put flowers in their hair, and claimed to be close to nature. Drugs, free love, and music were part of their freedom fests. Young people lived in housing arrangements that, by their parents' standards, were improper: communes of mixed families, unmarried couples living together, and men and women friends sharing housing.

Forty years later the new lifestyles of the 1960s are not unusual at all. Nobody cares who lives with whom in whatever housing arrangement. Housing choices are usually based on practical considerations rather than moral principles or propriety. Standards for acceptable language have relaxed, and the F-word has become an everyday word. Magazines like *Playboy* no longer need to be hidden away, and movies have become more explicit about sex, violence, and vulgarity. Boomers broke loose from the rules their parents had made for them.[7]

There were many legitimate social complaints in the 1960s, but we are distorting history if we pretend that youth culture was about general civic righteousness and a common commitment to democratic ideals. Numerous causes were being promoted, each with its own focus, a language of particular complaints, and a streak of personal self-interest. It was an era of

7. Supreme Court of the United States, "FCC v. Fox Television Stations." Epstein, "The Obscenity Business." Rembar, "Obscenity—Forget It."

ideology with many activist groups asserting their own agenda built around a single theme of protest against a particular form of injustice. What the participants in each particular movement had was a cause that was invested with the energy of their own convictions. What many of them lacked was concern for the freedoms of others.

- There was classism among feminists. Many of the women leading protests already had the benefits of a middle class life style. Poor women and minority women found it difficult to identify with the most visible and vocal feminists who had time for protests and consciousness-raising. Understanding the oppression of the homemaker was a far stretch for the poor sisters living on welfare or those who held more than one job in order to pay bills and keep their children fed.

- The militant civil rights movement was indifferent to the equal treatment of women. Within their own organization the Black Panthers did not allow women to hold roles of leadership. In the atmosphere of militarism and power, which some protest groups created, the treatment of women was often authoritarian and demeaning.

- There were racial tensions between minority groups. Though conscious of the wounds of anti-Semitism, many middle class Jewish families moved out when African American homeowners moved into their neighborhoods. Ethnic groups who themselves had suffered discrimination when they were new arrivals did not want to integrate the schools their children attended.

- The Flower Children were interested in a lighthearted life of ease, and that did not make them natural allies of factory workers, farm laborers, the latest wave of immigrants, or the poor who lived in urban slums. Few representatives from these latter groups were to be found at Woodstock, in the Village in New York, or on the streets of San Francisco during the Summer of Love.

- Blue-collar workers worried about money and jobs, and were critical of the corporations that employed them. Intellectuals in the university were critical of the same corporations. But blue-collar workers also despised intellectuals in the university whom they saw as living an easy life in which they could earn a living without breaking a sweat.[8]

8. Friedan, *The Feminine Mystique*. Marbley, "African-American Women's Feelings on Alienation From Third-wave Feminism." Greenberg, *Troubling the Waters: Black-Jewish Relations in the American Century*. Lasch, *The True and Only Heaven*.

And so it went. The freedom movements had their own form of sibling rivalry. If they did empower each other it was by the cumulative energy generated by so many things happening at once. It is far too simple to suggest that the unrest of the 1960s was created by the visionaries of justice all joining together to stand up against an oppressive Establishment. The youth culture of the 1960s culminated in a breakthrough time, but it was not heroic. Alvin Toffler in his book, *Future Shock*, which sold six million copies when it was released in 1970, explained the loss of consensus and rapid change in the culture of the United States as a result of "too much change in too short a time."[9]

Today Boomers draw strange looks from their grandchildren when the old folks tell the young folks the stories of the 1950s. Young people today can barely imagine that there were public drinking fountains from which African Americans were not allowed to drink. The idea of women's dormitories that were locked down each night at ten o'clock strikes them as absurd. They are stunned that young women would sneak off and risk their lives getting back alley abortions rather than admit to their families and friends that they were having sex. They cannot comprehend that anyone believed the public service films telling young people that if they smoked pot they would go insane.[10]

No doubt times have changed. Our habits and lifestyles have changed. Our rules of etiquette have changed inasmuch as there are far fewer of them overall, and new ones that are defined by political correctness have replaced the old ones. Our collective commitment to the traditional ideals of liberty has also changed. Liberty once meant that no group be allowed to impose its view on all others, and that no group with power be allowed to suspend the civil rights of a group with less power. The idea of license, which has been added to our understanding of freedom and liberty, means that no individual should make judgments about any other individual's choices, because what someone else does is not your concern unless it violates your own freedom.

Forty years into our experiment with freedom we are beginning to see more clearly the impact of our choices. We set our course, and we are still trying to sort it out. In our individual lives we try to decide what does matter and what does not, but this is complicated by the fact that we are

---

9. Toffler, *Future Shock*, 9.

10. This 1936 film is known as *Reefer Madness* or *Tell Your Children*.

uncertain about what we truly believe. Our ambivalence about conviction is linked to our understanding of freedom.

Culture is the mirror in which we see ourselves. It is the frame in which we draw conclusions about the ways in which we are like everyone else, and it is also the frame in which each one of us draws conclusions about how we are distinct from everyone else. We look to culture for perspective, but it mirrors back to us ambiguity about truth and uncertain boundaries to our freedoms. We are confused. We don't know where to begin.

Does being free release us to become a fully developed person, a healthy person, a good person, a productive person, and a happy person? The society in which we seek our personal fulfillment has become increasingly uncertain, while at the same time our freedoms have become increasingly unbounded. Among all the possibilities from which we are free to make our choices, how do we decide what we want?

5

Is Freedom an Illusion?

Freedom's just another word for nothing left to lose.

—JANIS JOPLIN[1]

THE CONVICTIONS ABOUT FREEDOM, individual license, and tolerance that took their roots as the Boomers were entering adulthood formed social attitudes for the next forty years. We thought that breaking loose from the oppression of the past would prepare us for the Age of Aquarius, which was envisioned as a time of peace, love, harmony, sympathy, and trust. Negativity toward others would fade away. Minds and spirits would be liberated from the shackles of the past. Unbridling the urgings of our nature would lead us to a better place. The Age of Aquarius did not dawn.[2]

Instead there have been other developments that have made managing our freedoms more difficult than we ever expected. In our infatuation with freedom we became confused about the extent of our personal responsibility. While reflexively we think freedom is a good thing, we have had to face the possibility that freedom can be destructive if our belief in it allows us to blunder forward with no regard for consequences.

1. Joplin, "Me and Bobbie McGee."
2. MacDermot, "Aquarius."

SOCIAL SCIENCE AND FREEDOM

In the 1960s social scientists in the United States were demonstrating that individuals are shaped by the circumstances of their surroundings. The methods upon which behavioral scientists depended were those that had been modeled for them in the natural sciences. Along with this trend, the rhetoric used to describe human actions was heavily influenced by the technical language of biology and engineering. Scientists described the way people behave as responses to factors that trigger, program, or condition them. In the new sciences of human behavior, moral judgment and individual character were concepts that no longer seemed fitting. Conscience? That became a questionable idea. Virtue? The idea seemed irrelevant.[3]

In a landmark study of obedience Stanley Milgram researched compliance to authority. The experimenter persuaded participants to deliver electric shocks when their partners on a task made mistakes. Gradually the level of shock was increased, and even though the instrument panel warned that the levels were dangerous many participants continued to shock their partners. The participants in Milgram's experiments were not being threatened or coerced; they were volunteers, and it appeared that they were acting freely. They had agreed to be in the experiment, and when they were instructed by the experimenter to deliver the shocks, they willingly went along. Although the participants did not know it, the experiment was a simulation and they were not actually delivering shocks. Had the setup involved real shocks, however, there is every reason to believe the participants would have gone ahead and delivered them to their partners anyway.

Milgram's experiment got wide news coverage. It shocked the public. Among social scientists there was less surprise because many theorists had already given up thinking that ideas like conscience or character were helpful for understanding why people behave as they do. At a minimum they seemed to be concepts beyond the reach of science. Some were willing to go the extra step of suggesting that these old fashioned ideas were mere illusion, and that humans are nothing more than complex animals.

Reviews of Milgram's research became standard content in Introductory Psychology texts, and millions of college students in the United States were taught about it. In society generally scientists were promoted as the experts who really understand why people behave as they do. Now, nearly fifty years later, behavioral scientists still believe that: "More than any other

---

3. Delgado, *Physical Control of the Mind.* Skinner, *Beyond Freedom and Dignity.*

investigation of its time, Milgram's work demonstrated the overwhelming power of situational variables."[4] Social science teachers, students, and researchers began to accept that human will and character are matters about which we can know little, if anything, scientifically. They are not concepts that help us understand how people behave under the pressure of circumstances.[5]

Social science research was pointing in two contradictory directions. These two conclusions were shaping the mind of the student reading a textbook, a citizen reading about behavioral research in the newspaper, and a teacher or parent taking a course in behavioral management. On the one hand research suggested that people are not responsible for their actions because their behavior is controlled by outside forces. On the other hand research was suggesting that the behavioral scientist has the power to control people by engineering their circumstances.

The election cycle in the United States illustrates this conflicted view of ourselves. It is a recurring ritual that stirs up our desire to believe we control the democratic process with votes. As we watch the process unfold, however, we begin to fear that we may be pawns on the chessboard of the political game. Are we at the mercy of the king-makers who know how to manipulate us? We are measured by pollsters, second-guessed by strategists, and manipulated by advertising and press releases. By Election Day we are not sure who chooses the outcome of the election. Do we control it with our puny little votes, or do those who know how to talk us out of our votes by playing with our minds engineer the outcome?[6]

The same split of perception has worked its way into social attitudes. On the one hand behavioral science puts the spotlight on the importance of altering social conditions so people will behave more humanely: a moral warning to a complacent society about its collective responsibility. On the other hand the findings of behavioral science feed resentment on the part of those who feel exploited in a big system of unmanageable circumstances. It has become a reason to deny personal responsibility for our choices when unfortunate things happen. From both the individual and the social perspectives it is difficult to sort out what it means *to be free*.

4. Milgram, *Obedience to Authority*. Burger, "Replicating Milgram: Would People Still Obey Today?"

5. Benjamin and Simpson, "The Power of the Situation," 17. Bem and Funder, "Predicting More of the People More of the Time."

6. Dan Ariely, *Predictably Irrational.*

WHO'S RESPONSIBLE AND WHERE DOES THE BUCK STOP?

If we are only as good (or bad) as our circumstances, then moral authority falls to those who can control circumstances. This is a significant problem for behavioral scientists. In the language of traditional morality we can talk of people being moral, but we cannot apply the idea of moral responsibility in the same way to circumstances. Circumstances do not have a conscience. They do not have memories. They cannot learn. Circumstances cannot make choices, and they do not make moral judgments. Assigning moral responsibility requires identifying persons who are moral agents.[7]

A split view of freedom engenders a split view of responsibility. If actions are controlled by circumstances, then those who can manipulate the circumstances are the moral agents: government, corporations, and institutional leaders. Those who are manipulated by circumstances, the simple people who do not understand what is happening to them and would not have the power to change their circumstances even if they did, are not responsible for their actions and choices. Left to the individual is the challenge of determining to become a controller or to submit to being one of the controlled.

Framed in this way theories developed by behavioral scientists create two classes of people: the controlled and the controlling or knowledge class. For a new generation rallying around the promises of freedom and equality, the idea of an oligarchy composed of the knowledge class was both an unsettling threat and an attractive escape from responsibility. On the one hand it is offensive to think that we are puppets dancing at the will of those who hold the strings. On the other hand it is tempting to point to the power of circumstances and shift blame to those in power when we ourselves trip up.

We blame others for setting us up for our mistakes: bad parents, bad teachers, bad spouses, bad bosses, and bad politicians. Apparently we think they are responsible. In the next breath we are ready to defend our freedoms as if we are beyond responsibility. Some motorcycle riders insist they should be free to ride without helmets if they like, even though the costs of long-term care after head injuries is drawn from an insurance pool into which everyone else pays. There are many smokers willing to blame the tobacco companies for their nicotine addictions. Overweight consumers

---

7. Humphreys, "AACU Announces National Initiative on Fostering Personal and Social Responsibility in Today's College Students." Tavris and Aronson, *Mistakes Were Made (But Not by Me).*

blame fast food restaurants for making servings too large and advertisers for making them too attractive. Who makes the choices? Do we make them, or are they made for us?

FREE TO GO TO THE LIMITS

Boomers resonated to the lyrics of Marlo Thomas encouraging them: "There's a land that I see where the children are free."[8] Among other things being free meant that boys are free to cry or play with dolls; girls are free to be pilots or presidents. Sung by children's voices it seemed so innocent and true. The freedom to which the song appeals is behavioral freedom that allows us to stand out from the crowd and do something different than is expected.

Is freedom a value in and of itself? Can we separate it from all other considerations? Are we willing to say that the expression of freedom is a good as it stands? Freedom of expression protects a variety of opinions. Increasingly it also protects a wide diversity of actions. When we are marching in step with others, following life patterns which are ordinary and familiar, we do not know if we are free or managed. We are most confident of our freedoms when we defy the limits.

Viewers of cable television were entertained when comedian George Carlin defiantly used the seven no-no words on television. Audiences bought tickets to listen to him name and mimic physical functions that normally are considered private. He was allowed to ridicule minorities, persons with physical challenges, and the aged.

A touring group called the *Sex Workers Art Show* has been allowed to put on its events in some campus facilities. Included in the show is a rendition of "America the Beautiful" which is played while a transvestite kneels on the stage with a lit sparkler protruding from his behind.

Tipper Gore, wife of then United States Senator Al Gore, purchased music for her daughter only to discover the lyrics contained references to exhibitionism and pedophilia. She joined with other parents to ask the music industry to label recordings so that prior to purchase parents could identify if they contained violence, reference to the occult, idealization of alcohol and drug use, or sexually explicit lyrics. Frank Zappa, the rock musician, called this "censorship" and printed a "warning guarantee" on his record labels. It said: "In some socially retarded areas religious fanatics and

8. Thomas, "Free to Be You and Me."

ultra-conservative political organizations violate your First Amendment rights by attempting to censor rock and roll albums."

The artist Andres Serrano produced a photograph of a crucifix in a bottle of his own urine. He called it *Piss Christ*. His work was funded by the National Endowment for the Humanities, which is one of the channels through which tax dollars support the arts. Some critics of Serrano's work argue that the desecration of a sacred symbol was not an appropriate use of tax dollars. Others called these complaints a form of censorship and repression.

In Jena, Louisiana nooses were used in displays of racial intimidation. There were copycat incidents. When a noose was hung on the office door of a professor at Columbia University Teacher's College the President of the College called it "a hateful act, which violates every . . . social norm." Lawmakers in the State of Maryland initiated a proposal to make the use of nooses in racial intimidation a hate crime. In debate of the bill one of the lawmakers asked: "Do you no longer have the right to hate?"

After a number of incidents during which persons falsely claimed military service and acts of valor, the United States Congress passed the Stolen Valor Act. Xavier Alvarez was charged and convicted under this act because he claimed that he had served in combat as a Marine and that he was awarded a medal of honor. In a process of appeals the United States Supreme Court has been asked to make a judgment about whether the right to lie in this way falls under the protections of free speech. Some news organizations have argued that it should.[9]

Does commitment to the value of free expression mean all expressions of freedom have at least some merit because they prove we are not repressed? I want to be very clear that I am not suggesting a roll back in freedoms. We create social and legal latitude for others to make choices that we ourselves judge to be unfortunate. We tolerate this dissonance out of the conviction that the constructive uses of freedom must not be stifled. In the spirit of democracy we leave room for error because we prefer to err on the side of freedom, and the legal freedoms we defend are far broader than the moral principles to which we ourselves subscribe.

9. Zoglin, "Rebel at the Mike." Taylor, "The University Has No Clothes." Feldman, "Frank Zappa vs. Tipper Gore." Casey, "Sacrifice, Piss Christ, and Liberal Excess." Fantz, "Noose incidents." Kessler, "Columbia Professors Get Images of Swatikas, Noose in Mail." Wyatt, "Nooses May Be Added to Md. Hate Crime Law." Liptak, "Justices Appear Open to Affirming Medal Law."

In order to protect freedoms we endure some cultural damage. But there is a new question with which we grapple: Do I have a right to be protected from someone else's abuse of freedom? If freedom, understood as license, means that being progressive requires us to pretend that all uses of freedom are of equal merit, then our sense of discernment may be eroding. Our sense of freedom may be closing in on itself.

We owe each other the protections of freedom, but we do not owe each other blind admiration for nonconformity. Certain expressions of freedom do not contribute to the quality of our common life, and others can lead to tragedy. If we are not willing both to protect freedom and be outspoken about the downside of some things we are free to do, then we are far less free than we think.

When internet freedom includes instructions for constructing bombs it is dangerous. Art that debases others is antisocial. Unlaundered language can do damage; that is why there are rules in institutions about the use of racist and sexist epithets, even though in private life people are free to use them and many do. Thoughtless people can be self-destructive. Freedom expressed without the constraints of any other principles of constructive behavior may result in cultural vandalism. We may not have the right to inhibit others from doing these things, but that should not inhibit us from saying what we think about their choices.

In the 1970s the Sex Pistols captured public attention for a time. While they were waiting in an airport they vomited on other passengers in the waiting area. The Pistols were in the news again when Sid murdered his girlfriend. Not long after, while out on bail, he died of a drug overdose. The measure of their freedom was how far they dared to go before anyone would stop them. They were shocking and bizarre. That was their intention. What is most remarkable is how many fans they gathered in the process.

There were numerous other rock stars like the Pistols, willing to dance on the edge of destruction. Decades later fans remain fascinated by the Forever 27 Club whose members, all well-known entertainers, died by age twenty-seven of drug overdoses, suicide, and accidents. Among the best known are Brian Jones of the Rolling Stones, Jimi Hendrix, Janis Joplin, Jim Morrison of the Doors, Curt Cobain of Nirvana, and Amy Winehouse. There are over a dozen others. It seems they were important to their fans because living without limits is one of the fantasies of freedom, but were they really free?[10]

10. Savage, *England's Dreaming: Sex Pistols and Punk Rock*. Wikipedia, *"27 Club."*

IS LICENSE WITHOUT LIMITS REALLY FREEDOM?

In a free society there is considerable latitude allowed for us to develop our own rules for living. Most of us do not choose to use all of our freedoms. For example, as long as you are in your own home (not in a public place or behind the wheel of a car) you are free to drink as much as you please. However, pressing that limit to the point of alcohol poisoning may risk your life or drive away your family. We may neglect our children as long as we do not beat, starve, or pimp them because the minimum required by law is far less than they need. But who would honor that neglect as a fitting expression of freedom?

Part of being a healthy person is learning to set limits to our freedom. We may be free now to use the F-word in good company, and we may not have to hide the fact that we smoked pot or did a few lines of coke when we were young. But are we now freer to do good things than we were in the past? Do we have more power to affect our destiny positively? Do we know how to live better with our neighbors? Are we really in charge of our freedom?

Freedom depletes itself when it becomes a license to violate all other principles with no regard, and freedom becomes skinny when it is so intent on unlimited expression that it leaves no place for a life shared with others. We can elect to exercise our own personal freedom in ways that are constructive rather than destructive, in ways that develop a more civil and respectful society rather than a savage and brutal one. To do that we need to believe in the power of our own personal responsibility, so that acting in the interests of others is understood as an expansion of freedom rather than a limit on it.

We got used to thinking that all opinions are relative and that we are free to do as we please because we are free individuals. But now we are discovering that freedom is more than an individual matter. If my lifestyle warms my globe it warms yours too. If the rich waste the world's resources, it is not they but the poor who suffer most from the shortfalls. If workers a half world away use cheap or inferior materials in products, our children may be harmed by them. It may be difficult for you to do much about my choices if they are freely mine to make. To some degree we are at each other's mercy, and that means that sometimes your freedom endangers me, and mine can endanger you.

Freedom does not stand by itself, nor does my exercise of it matter only to me. The ideas of freedom which we devised in the 1960s need to be redefined if we hope to come to terms with the realities of a shrinking globe and rapid reactions in an age of connectivity. We need cooperation. We need an expansion of our consciousness to include concern for others. That requires a new take on freedom because without the ability to form community, we will not be able to resolve the most challenging problems that now threaten our world. Has our view of personal license equipped us to think about freedom together?

Some time ago I was riding in a taxi through a busy section of Beijing. The driver was one of the new generation of young Chinese eager to practice English. There was plenty of opportunity because we were stopped in traffic for several minutes at a time. I asked him what he thinks of the United States. He told me he likes Americans who come to China and bring work. Then he went on to say that he worries about the United States economy because China does business with the United States. I asked him how he knows about the United States. He told me he knows from the internet.

A taxi driver in Beijing is watching us, and I am watching China. Shortly after arriving home I read about an epidemic of AIDS in rural China. It seems the infection was spread through contaminated blood collected from poor donors in rural clinics where incorrect procedures had been used. Disease does not stop at national boundaries. Not long after that I read about contaminated food products being produced in China. The production stream of food manufacture also crosses national boundaries. Whether we are friends or enemies, we are neighbors. Our choices matter to each other.

If we think we are free to act as we please and do as we please without consequences, we are deluding ourselves. The taxi driver in Beijing cannot escape the consequences of my actions, and I cannot escape the consequences of his. It is impossible for you to detach yourself from me, and for me to detach myself from you because we are inescapably interdependent. Are we still free?

RESPONSIBLE FREEDOM

It will require some ingenuity to refocus our vision of freedom in an age of interdependence. Convinced that freedom is license, Boomers revoked many of the obligations of social responsibility. Social science researchers of the era also minimized personal responsibility by attributing human behavior to situational factors. Meanwhile many persons in the youth culture acted out their freedom through expansive self-expression. We have continued to be confused about the extent of our freedom, the degree to which we are formed by factors over which we have no control, and the extent of our responsibility.

At its best freedom is an ongoing process by which we creatively extend our boundaries and then mindfully sharpen our conscience to adjust to the new ways of doing things. The difference between freedom and chaos rests on our willingness to be responsible. Forty years ago when Boomers made the claim to personal freedom they thought greater freedom would turn them loose from unnecessary restrictions carried over from the past. It was an exhilarating and optimistic time. They thought freedom was theirs for claiming it.

Now forty years later we see that along with our freedom comes responsibility, and responsibility takes discipline. But discipline challenges our sense of freedom because we do not like being answerable to anyone but ourselves. At the same time in order to accomplish good we need to know in what we anchor our own personal sense of meaning, and we need to be clear about the shared principles that support our collective sense of justice and right. Choices for freedom and responsibility are ours, but by what standard will we measure our choices, and how will we communicate our intentions? We are tangled in freedom.

6

Free Opinions

The rule is perfect: *In all matters of opinion
our adversaries are insane.*

—MARK TWAIN[1]

OUR CULTURE IS LIKE Humpty Dumpty. We knocked it down, and there is no way of putting it back together again in the form it once was. Some see that as a mission accomplished, and others see that as the loss of a good past. One of the most challenging features of the cultural shifts that have occurred since the 1960s is the scatter of opinions. There is a widespread view that everyone is entitled to have opinions, that all views fall under the protection of free expression, and that very little may be said about their relative merits.

The right to have opinions has become a central tenet in our culture's emotional bill of rights. As individuals claim for themselves the right to have their own opinions, the social tradeoff is to give others the same right, at least most of the time. It is nearly impossible to question someone who claims the right to have an opinion, just as it is almost unimaginable to say to anyone "you have no right to be free."

There are three common variants of the claim to freedom of opinion: cautious individualism, ideological empowerment, and comfortable

---

1. Twain, *Christian Science*, 41.

hedonism. They are built on the same basic assumptions, and each in its own way has acquired social status as a self-evident truth.

CAUTIOUS INDIVIDUALISM

If they ever gave up being forever young, cautious individualists might have to call themselves the "Uncertain Generation." They do not trust that they are entitled to say what they believe with certainty because they are afraid of being dogmatic. They are persuaded that among the enlightened, truth is always granted a status no stronger than that of a courteous opinion.

Cautious individualists are particularly careful when they find themselves in a context where others might pass judgment on them. They hesitate because they do not want to impose their views on others, and they are concerned that their beliefs might not be respected. Admitting conviction makes them vulnerable. Cautious individualists remain silent rather than create the awkwardness of being out of sync with people who are friends, neighbors, coworkers, family members, or the comfortable majority.

The more valuable a conviction is, the more uncomfortable it can be to discover that others reject it. Being vulnerable about things that matter only a little is easy. Being vulnerable about things that matter a great deal is far more difficult. Opinions become weighty when we are discussing the meaning of death with someone who has cancer, justice with someone whose child was driving drunk and caused a fatal car crash, or the fairness of the death penalty with someone whose daughter was raped by a habitual offender. When it comes to putting their cards on the table cautious individualists are willing to voice opinions but cautious about exposing beliefs.

If you ask cautious individualists what they believe, they have an easier time telling you what they do not believe. If you press them for conviction they are likely to become shy and tell you they would rather keep it to themselves. That is a courteous way of telling you they would rather not give you the opportunity to criticize what they think. They are defensive about being attacked, and they are almost as defensive about being persuaded. They can make an uncomfortable conversation come to a halt by declaring, "You're entitled to your own opinion."

Our cultural confusion about opinions has created a spiritual vacuum, and many in our culture suffer from *spiritual shame*. Those things we are deeply committed to are also the things we hide. Shame is a feeling that lies deep. It tampers with the core of our self-worth. It leaves us feeling that what we are, the things we cannot change, are outside the bounds of what entitles us to respect from others. While we may proclaim that everyone is entitled to have opinions, we may also secretly believe that those who do not hold the same opinions we do are a threat to us. This double bind triggers our shame. Behaviorally we are tolerant, but intellectually we are judgmental, and personally we are timid.

Shame is an inner conflict that gets tangled up with our own truth. And spiritual shame is a particular form of it that robs us of confidence in our convictions when others do not agree. Spiritual shame can make us uneasy even when we cast our lot with something we believe is good and right and true. Each time we long for certainty but do not feel entitled to have it, the ghost of shame creeps up and shakes a finger of rebuke at us.

Despite the rhetoric of freedom cautious individualists are isolated in their opinions. If we hold convictions in silence do we feel stronger? If we drift toward a passive stance that does not bother with conviction at all, won't we feel empty? Are we really safer if we do not know what others think?

I had an interesting conversation over lunch with an intelligent professional woman, one whom I hold in high regard. Over our salads I told her my views of adolescents and music. I expressed concern about whether daily exposure to violent lyrics played through ear buds is an unhealthy way to program the adolescent brain that is still in a state of rapid development. I explained to her that I am interested in the use of certain types of music for stress reduction, and that also has led me to think about certain other types of music as possibly provoking stress or even seeding aggression.

I could tell that my friend did not want to agree with me. We both have raised children who were free to listen to the music they chose. We were open-minded Baby Boomers, and our children enjoyed a great deal of latitude. First she cautioned me that limiting adolescents too much is not usually effective. I agreed with her that teens are more likely to select their music based on the choices of their friends than the advice of their parents. That aside, I asked her what she thought about the impact of violent lyrics. She responded by reminding me that my concern about it is "just my opinion."

It is my opinion, and I own that. The peculiar thing about this conversation was that I could not get my friend to tell me her opinion, nor could I get her to tell me what she thought of mine. She just bowed out. There were things that were not said in our conversation. Neither of us admitted that when we have strong sentiments about a matter, it feels dismissive to have it set aside as merely an opinion. And neither of us bothered to observe that usually when people agree with each other neither says, "Oh well, these are just our opinions, aren't they?"

The way our conversation ended points to a certain shallowness in conversations that are bound up by the rules that govern the freedom of opinions. In the end she thought her opinions were important because they were hers, and I thought mine were important because they were mine. We were stuck almost as soon as we began, because we were dealing with opinions. The rules of etiquette that entitle each of us to hold our own opinions hijacked the conversation, isolating us from each other.

IDEOLOGICAL EMPOWERMENT

Not everyone buys into intellectual relativism; some opt out of the contract to be tactful about the opinions of others while not being pushy about their own. They are tired of the dance of uncertainty and have decided to speak out. Their assertions are a matter of will, an expression of power. We see this in the face-offs of talk television that display noisy arguments and no effort by anyone to listen to the other side.

Friedrich Nietzsche outlined a process something like this. He suggested that after all certainty is lost, there would be two sorts of persons. One is the type who bungles along with what is left of the old rules for civility, the nice person who is predictable. The other is the "man who has gone beyond" (*Übermensch*) and asserts power by rising above the rest. When power looms large it appears that only these two choices remain: fight for self-interest or consent to be an underdog.[2]

The shift away from cooperation and toward power surfaced during the past four decades as we lost shared assumptions that had previously structured cooperation. During times of conflict people are drawn to ideology. They organize their views around a few central ideas, and then they use those views to defend the interests of their own group. In an age of ideology public rhetoric is abundant with words that end in *ism: sexism, ageism, classism, racism, fundamentalism, globalism, environmentalism, militarism,* and others. The worth of anyone else's opinion is measured by whether it is a support or a challenge.

2. Nietzsche, *Thus Spake Zarathustra.*

In the context of an ideological battle what is the worth of an opinion? In 2005 Lawrence Summers, who was then President of Harvard University, got into a struggle with some members of the faculty because he suggested that the predominance of men in the sciences might be due to a difference in innate ability between men and women. There was an immediate reaction. Though he qualified his statement and apologized for his formulation of it, the gaffe was out.[3]

Lawrence Summers thought that in the context of the university he was free to speak his mind. Among his defenders were those who, though they did not agree with his view, did believe he should be free to make his views public. His most outspoken critics, however, did not think that Summers had the right to speak his views freely because a person holding one of the highest positions of power in the university could not be trusted if he held negative opinions about women. There was too much at stake. A sufficient number of his colleagues withdrew their support, and he was forced out. In a battle of ideologies Summers and his supporters lost the power struggle.

It is not my intent here to join in the debate about Lawrence Summers, but it is instructive to look at what happens when powerful people, without a common base of agreement, hold opposing opinions. The faculty at Harvard represents a collection of different views, many based on the personal interests of those who hold them. Who then can determine what may or may not be said? It is determined by a coalition of the majority. It is determined by power.

In the past university debates took place in the context of general agreement. The common ground was reason. Today there are some who would call trust in reason just another ideology, i.e., *rationalism*. In the intellectual community, they would argue, the politics of the university always existed, and the idea of a community guided by reason was a pretense to cover the ambitions of those who were in charge. Increasingly the university has become a place where the proponents of various rights joust with each other. Sometimes when the battle gets heated, it is no longer just about opinions. Those who cannot line up the support of colleagues are made to leave.

James Watson, the Nobel Prize winner famous for his work on DNA, was relieved of his position doing research at Cold Springs Laboratory because he made politically incorrect comments. He suggested that Africans

3. Finder et al., "President of Harvard Resigns, Ending Stormy 5-year Tenure."

are less intelligent than Europeans. Immediately many universities followed the action of Cold Springs and withdrew their invitations to have Watson speak. The mistakes Watson made were not in the laboratory. He headed a laboratory that published more than 1500 scientific papers, and his group paved the way to new research in many significant areas. At the time Watson made his objectionable statement his research was as careful as ever.[4]

Watson's mistake was that he made comments that were politically unacceptable. Other intellectuals did not want to be associated with him or appear in any way to condone his views. He became a pariah and left his position in ignominy. His accomplishments as a scientist did not insure his right to say whatever he pleased. His position of prestige came with an obligation to maintain an especially high standard of responsibility for his public comments, and he failed to live up to that professional expectation.

Some people are allowed to say disrespectful things about others in the intellectual community; others are not. It is hard to imagine that a student at Harvard would be penalized for making sexist statements, for defending pornography that debases women, or for actually treating a woman with disrespect at a party. Are these matters of ethics? Freedom of speech? Ultimately they seem to be matters of power. In the hierarchy of the university, students do not have much power. Their freedom of opinion is less threatening than that of the president or a world-class scientist.

Ideology is a formulation of ideas that gets us what we want. Reasons are less important than rights, and in an arena where that is acceptable, power based on who talks fastest, loudest, and longest also often determines who gets the last word. It does not matter that views are just opinions. In the contest of ideologies the most assertive will win, and that determines what does and does not happen.

THE COMFORTABLE HEDONIST

Individualists who are wary of conviction may be a holdover from the orderly social structures of the 1950s. Outspoken ideology and fights about rights do not seem unfamiliar after the upheavals of the 1960s. Now there is a new rhetoric of opinions. It is a hedonic view. In this most recent rhetoric of opinions you are entitled to hold any opinion you like for no other reason than that you are *comfortable* with it. No need to build a case, demonstrate that your opinion is reasonable, or show that you have assembled evidence

4. BBC. "Lab suspends DNA Pioneer Watson."

for it. Opinions are matters of personal taste. They are devices for expressing yourself, and you are entitled to use them as you please.

The freedom to hold whatever opinions we like is an article in an emotional bill of rights that has taken hold in the culture of the United States. It is based on the belief that all individuals have the right to make choices, and that they have the *right to be comfortable* with the choices they make. The rhetorical claim to freedom of opinion is a conversation manager. What is implied when you assume that your opinions are as good as anyone else's while at the same time not granting everyone else's opinions the status of being as good as yours? As odd as it might sound stated outright, that is not an unusual way of thinking in a context of unquestioned self-interest.

Some notions about everybody having a good opinion may have come from teachers who used it to get students to participate in classroom discussion. All students are entitled to put their bit in, and in order to keep the discussion going the teacher does not weigh in on any particular position. After the 1960s there were new rules about teachers not making students feel bad by embarrassing them in class, and in that educational atmosphere questioning the unformed opinions of students was considered authoritarian and repressive.

Calling something "just an opinion" is more sophisticated than telling someone to shut up. The idea that everyone is free to have an opinion is a *comfort view*. Comfort food is something we reach for when, rather than truly hungry, we just need something to make us feel good. A comfort view is an idea we reach for when, feeling uncomfortable with debate, we try to find a way to get out of it. Comfort views do not add much to the dialogue, but they do make us feel better for the present. They do not deepen our understanding of the issues or help us find common ground, but they are a way to relieve the tension when we feel backed into a corner.

Many intelligent and well-intentioned people use the claim to freedom of opinions as a comfort view. When we toss the view of free opinions into a conversation it is usually because we do not want to be bothered by the requirement that a view worth supporting is one that has been substantiated. Neither do we want to be bound by a rule that says an idea that has been thought through and found flawed is not worth keeping. The expression *Whatever!* is the new way of reducing a conversation to mere opinion. It is really a way of saying, "Go ahead and think what you want because it doesn't matter."

DO WE REALLY BELIEVE ALL OPINIONS ARE EQUAL?

The right of opinions is built into our language and thought so that we have a shortcut way of dealing with differences and conflict. In some cases this choice for peaceful co-existence has merit, but it carries a risk of keeping our interactions at a trivial level. There are matters we need to deal with, and to do that we need dialogue. Opting out with an appeal to freedom of opinion leaves us in gridlock.

My neighbor thinks it is acceptable to smoke in the car while he is driving our kids to soccer practice. I think that his behavior exposes his child and mine to secondhand smoke and it is unhealthy. We each have an opinion. I suppose we each are entitled to think about it through all the avenues, alleys, bends, and turns that we do. Then we come to a conclusion we call *an opinion*. Is that really as far as we can go? Can we be satisfied with that? What happens to the kids? Do I allow mine to ride in his car? When it comes to making wise choices, the comfort we find in the freedom of opinions is not a good place for the deliberations to end.

What is missing in each one of the interpretations of freedom of opinion is dialogue, real conversation in which we are free to speak, willing to hear, and committed to keep the exchange going until we come to a better place. Witness the talking heads on television who babble through each other about the day's issues. We often witness confrontations in which all parties claim the right to speak. Far less often do we witness exchanges in which all parties demonstrate thoughtful listening. And exchanges in which parties come to a better place are the least common of all.

There are those who would caution us that some issues will never be resolved no matter how long the dialogue continues. While that may be true in some instances, it will happen less often if we engage in dialogue. There will be fewer occasions in which the rush to a showdown results in polarization. It seldom works to eclipse the possibility of cooperation because the losers in the debate will not be silenced indefinitely. If the issue is of importance to them, the debate will be revived.

Did Boomers' pursuit of freedom exaggerate our separateness and independence? Did it distract us from a commitment to sustain a diverse culture with a readiness to exchange ideas and a will to cooperate? Is it possible to work together if we cannot talk together? Does this not require that we hold ourselves accountable for our own opinions, and that we be willing to measure them again after they have been challenged by new ideas or come into contact with perspectives vastly different from our own?

7

Tangled in Freedom

I'm empty and aching, and I don't know why.

—Paul Simon[1]

BABY BOOMERS ARE GROWING older, and observers of the generation, many of them Boomers themselves, are judging their performance. They still exhibit some of the immaturity of youth, thinking they are a special generation. Despite the forward moves they have made, however, the way their lives have turned out does not please them. They continue to be puzzled about the most basic human questions. What really matters? What makes life worthwhile?

To mark the 65th birthday of the oldest Baby Boomers the Pew Research Forum conducted an extensive survey of their opinions and attitudes. The research summary describes Boomers as "glum." They are discouraged about the direction the country is going, do not feel confident that their children and grandchildren will have what they need economically, do not trust their leaders, and worry that their communities and institutions are in decline. The report calls the Boomers the gloomiest generation.[2]

In addition to being gloomy many Boomers feel stuck. They acted out their sense of entitlement before they had learned to distinguish freedom to create from license to destroy. They questioned the foundations of truth

1. Simon, "America."
2. Pew Forum on Religion and Public Life, "Statistics on Religion in America."

and goodness so that convictions, including their own, began to look like flimsy opinions. They did away with associations and habits that were part of a traditional lifestyle because they thought they were burdensome. In many cases they made judgments without sorting through and distinguishing the wisdom of the ages from its failures. They ushered in an era in which growing older and accumulating wisdom were no longer honored. Young people no longer respect elders or consider them wise because they are likely to be out of touch with technology and the themes that are current, or so we think.

Boomers are not lazy. Nearly a third of them volunteer. They help with disaster relief, give hours to their local school, and stuff envelops for fundraisers and campaigns. Check out who is tending the booths and desks at community events. Many of the volunteers are Boomers. There is no question that the hours and labor they contribute are worthwhile. But these activities are not central to their lives. They do not help Boomers answer their deepest spiritual questions about the meaning of life.

Like everything else, causes are transitory. Disasters pass. Cam-paigns end. Even movements to bring about social change eventually become less interesting. Consider that there are far fewer feminists today than there were in the 1960s. What was a cause then is now a right. Our daughters take their freedoms for granted, and both they and we have turned to issues that seem more pressing. In order to ground our sense of meaning we need something deeper than today's activities or a current cause.

Boomers do not lack for social contacts, especially fleeting ones. If we choose we can be "around" people. We can go to the coffee shop and hang out with others who are busy at work on their laptops or engrossed in what they are reading. The library has lounge areas with comfy chairs, and we are welcome to stay as long as we like in the company of others who are quietly gathered there. We can spend hours updating our own Facebook pages and browsing the latest posted by those who have "friended" us.

All these intersections of our lives create an illusion of social contact, but they do not create communities in which we share our deepest concerns. We do not know much about the people we meet at work, at the health club, in the grocery store, or any of the other places at which we spend a few minutes or a few hours of our day. We know nothing about what they think in their most thoughtful moments, and they do not know that about us. In our search for meaning we are alone.

Now and then something happens that jars us to consciousness. That wakes us up. Often they are momentous events that come into our national consciousness. On September 11, 2001 we knew what was on everyone's mind, and we could talk about it with anyone we encountered that day. The massacre in Tucson that wounded Gabrielle Giffords also was an event that captured national attention. The nation watched to see if she would survive. People were touched by her tragedy and the agonizing loss of those who were killed or wounded in the attack on her. Suddenly millions of Americans felt connected to people about whom they had not known just a few days earlier.

These days of national shock and reflection are exceptions. They create occasions on which public figures call us back to our better selves. Their speeches appeal to us to be neighborly, civil, brave, and hopeful. Briefly speakers dare to point to the sacred by quoting from the Bible, petitioning that God will bless America, and advising us to pray for each other. The stories they tell of courage and loss bring tears to our eyes. Even the voices of brave men quiver as they speak of these things.

Then days pass, and we do not know how to make what we have experienced in these poignant moments part of our usual horizon of meaning. It is hard to share old news. In the end most of us, along with millions of others who have witnessed these stunning events, are spectators. We do not know how to live our own lives differently after witnessing something stunning. Much of what makes up our own lives remains the same, and our daily activities go back to being what they were before.

Boomers distanced themselves from the traditions and environments in which earnest dialogue used to occur on a small and personal scale. They scaled down the importance of neighborhoods, religious congregations, extended families, and the other associations in which people knew each other by name and communicated face to face. These encumbrances were shed like leftovers of the past. The "young forever" generation wanted to live in the present and be tuned to the future. They did not want relationships that entailed obligations. If they lived entirely in the present, defying age and refusing to grow up, they assumed they would not have to burden themselves with questions about life's meaning. Focusing on themselves and what was immediately important to them personally, they thought, would have meaning enough.

SELF WITH CAPITAL LETTERS

Self is what remained after the Boomer generation stripped away many of the stabilizing structures and traditional beliefs that had helped previous generations define themselves. While scientists were convincing us that our planet and our solar system are not the center of the universe, we were also being assured by the gurus of our age that each of us has an ego that can be our own center of meaning. We became islands of Self (with a capital letter). Virginia Satir, a family therapist who was popular during the 1960s and 70s, put it this way: "I am Me. . . . Everything that comes out of me is authentically mine, because I alone chose it. . . . Because I own all of me, I can become intimately acquainted with me. By so doing, I can love me . . ."[3]

The elevation of self allowed each of us to assert shamelessly: "nothing should ever be more important to me than I am to myself." Unfortunately as our sense of entitlement and self-importance grew, we became entangled in our redesigned freedoms. As we became increasingly self-serving, we also became threatened by the selfishness of others, especially if it got in the way of getting for ourselves what we wanted.

In an essay about American culture written in the 1980s the social philosopher Robert Nisbet observed that many people are disconnected from the work they do, from the network of relationships in which they exist, from the communities in which they live, and from the ideas of the past that formed the collective experience that people shared with each other. He called this *alienation*. As this pattern was spreading among Americans, Nisbet observed: "the number increases of people who believe themselves to be powerless or who are chronically and irremediably bored with, cynical about, or uninterested in anything beyond their immediate selves and instant gratification of whatever narcissistic, hedonistic, and solipsistic needs arise in their selves."[4]

It is difficult for us to reach out beyond ourselves, to escape the haze of meaninglessness unless we have convictions and share them with others. But we are wary of shared convictions. We do not want to be entrapped by ideas imposed from the outside, and we do not want to be dominated by the controlling assertions of others. It is this predicament to which Nisbet points when he warns of solipsism and preoccupation with self. When Nisbet was writing he was echoing things that had been said much earlier by

---

3. Satir, Virginia Satir Quotes.

4. Nisbet, *Prejudices*, 11.

Alexis de Tocqueville. Writing nearly a century before the Boomers were born, he warned about an isolating sequence of moral shifts that begins with a breakdown of virtue in public life, then erodes morals in private life, and finally leaves every individual trapped within the self.[5]

The risk of self-centeredness is nothing new. But the Boomer experiment with it has significant features. Our move toward self-focus has been propagated by mass media, has been reinforced by the marketing of images that fuel consumerism, and has been made possible by living on credit. Our self-centeredness is also material and financial self-centeredness. It may be that the first decades of the new millennium will demonstrate through actual events that our ways of living have natural limits.

If we have nothing outside of ourselves that seems secure, and if we have only ourselves and our own interests to guide us, what really matters? This is a dilemma for our generation. The more tentative we are about the meaning of everything around us, the more we are left with only our own desires to weigh our actions. Our own ambitions are the bottom line. Knowing what we want and going after it without hesitation is the new definition of "integrity" or strong character.

Shortly after presidential candidate John Edwards admitted his affair with Rielle Hunter, CBS aired an interview with Hunter's good friend Pigeon O'Brien. Like a loyal friend O'Brien presented Hunter as a good person, talented, intelligent, and with "great integrity." The interviewer asked if Hunter had a struggle of conscience about the fact that she was having an affair with a married man, and in particular one whose wife was battling cancer. O'Brien replied: "I don't suppose we ever went into things on the conscience level. It wasn't for me to judge and she didn't want to put me in a position to judge her. We were girlfriends; we trusted one another's decisions."

It seems that the interviewer did not want to let O'Brien off the hook so easily. The conversation came back around to what Rielle Hunter thought of John Edward's wife and the commitments of their marriage. O'Brien admitted that her friend was fully aware of the significant role Elizabeth played in John's life:

> She's very aware of it. There are other circumstances—their affair, their connection, their love—that seemed to make it OK and comfortable for her to pursue the relationship with him. From the outside it doesn't look like we would make those same choices;

5. Quoted in ibid., 184.

she was comfortable making those choices and confident in those choices.[6]

This response fills in what Pigeon O'Brien meant by integrity. It refers to having a will, making choices independently, and feeling comfortable with them. It is the integrity of a self-defined individualist. Friends who accept this view of integrity do not interfere with each other. They accept that what others do is their own business.

It probably did not help Rielle Hunter or John Edwards to have their story blabbed in the news to millions of curious viewers, and public pressure did not help Elizabeth Edwards deal with this intimate betrayal while at the same time she was facing her own mortality. On the other hand it might have helped Rielle to have a few honest friends to help her see beyond her self-interest.

Having some honest friends might also have helped John Edwards, who now says of himself: "In the course of several campaigns I started to believe that I was special and became increasingly egocentric and narcissistic." Edwards is the sort of person Nisbet describes as alienated. Trapped in himself and lonely.[7]

THE FRAGILE SELF

As the Boomers age they face the greatest challenge to the omnipotent self around which they have built their lives. Those who measure the meaning of life in units of happiness, adventure, and pleasure begin to worry about what will keep them satisfied as they enter the inevitable process of decline. They are better at describing what makes them glum. They fear everything fragile and uncertain. Saul Bellow, one of the outstanding literary voices of the Boomer generation, said it well when his character, Herzog, mused:

> But what is the philosophy of this generation? Not God is dead, that point was passed long ago. Perhaps it should be stated Death is God. This generation thinks—and this is its thought of thoughts—that nothing faithful, vulnerable, fragile can be durable or have any true power. Death waits for these things as a cement floor waits for a dropping light bulb. The brittle shell of glass loses its tiny vacuum with a burst and that is it.[8]

6. Rodriguez, "Is Edwards Lying About Timeline of Affair?"
7. Ross, "Edwards Admits to Extramarital Affair."
8. Bellow, *Herzog*, 289–90.

Living in the moment and staying occupied with ourselves does not let us escape the growing evidence that we are bound by time. The self that in our youth we assumed would always be is the same self we now understand will only be for a limited time. All around us is evidence to remind us of our impermanence.

We witness others who meet their end. Some are those we love. Some are those we barely know. Some are those we only know as huge numbers reported as victims of a hurricane or an earthquake. Some drift away easily in their sleep surrounded by their families, and some go in great suffering or totally alone. Some we know about because we have seen those who grieve them on the glass screens of our televisions. Some we know because we have held them in our own arms, and now we can no longer. The story of last moments varies, but the outcome is the same. They are no longer here.

In all their variety these images of departure reflect to us the same message. Our own mortality. We are like Bellow's light bulb. Fragile. All facing that sliver in time when we make the transition from present to absent. From living to . . . and that second term is ineffable. It is a reality before which we are humble. We seem not able to grasp it. We cannot envision our total absence, the end of our own self, because we have only ever been here. Even if we are confident that our self continues in some other form or other dimension, we must admit that it does not continue as we know it now.

Making ourselves the center did not make our lives meaningful. Claiming for ourselves what we could to manage, spend, and enjoy did not satisfy us. Self-focused Boomers have remained childish. They lived in a big world they did not understand, demanded of it what they wanted, and now are utterly puzzled because they have not gotten from it what they expected.

The Self in isolation is fragile because it exists in a spiritual vacuum. Without a comprehensive story within which to understand ourselves we turn to the shopping bazaar of current ideas. Look at what is featured on the covers of magazines. Check out the self-help section of a bookstore: shelves of books offering advice about happiness, success, better relationships, organizing priorities, managing time, finding a spiritual path, and much more.

I have wondered while standing before those shelves what we think "self-help" means. Does it mean self-service? Do we really think we can find meaning on our own by reading a book? Or is it a challenge? Do we go to those shelves because we cannot find meaning on our own and are in tough straits? In any case, there are many interesting ideas to be found in the self-help section, but with so many from which to choose, how do we determine what we can confidently embrace?[9]

As we age we long for stories that have a scope greater than ourselves. We long for a personal story that weaves us together with other people and events beyond us. These are serious stories that express for us what the meaning of our lives has been. When I ask where I came from, I don't need to be reminded that I was born in Iowa. I want a better, deeper answer than that. When I wonder what the future will bring, I am looking for an answer more substantial than a reminder on my smartphone that I have appointments tomorrow and am flying to Atlanta next week. And when I am jolted by the evidence that there is suffering in the world, so many things that are not the way they should be, I need more assurance than the bumper sticker on a stranger's car that reads, "Shit Happens."

In his book, *The Cry for Myth*, the psychotherapist Rollo May describes a deep loneliness that comes not from the absence of people but from the absence of a shared and intuitively understood base of meaning. At the time May was writing in the 1990s, there was a great deal of optimism about progress, but read today we see that his words of caution were prescient:

> Many people in our day . . . are alone with no myths to guide them, no unquestioned rites to welcome them into community, no sacraments to initiate them into the holy—and there is rarely anything holy. *The loneliness of mythlessness is the deepest and least assuageable of all.* Unrelated to the past, unconnected with the future, we hang as if in mid-air.[10]

Left on our own we lack a starting place, a measure of meaning. We do not know how to get deeper than the passing curiosity we feel about an endless array of ideas that are "just opinions." We do not know how to create a coherent vision that allows us to place the ordinary events of today into the larger story of our lives, and then how to place the narrative of our individual lives into a story that is more enduring than we are.

This notion of a coherent picture is nothing new. Friedrich Nietzsche called it a horizon, the view that serves as the background against which we see everything else. There are many names by which we may choose to call it: myth, Weltanschauung, worldview, framework, horizon, unified theory,

9. McGee, *Self-Help Inc.: Makeover Culture in American Life.*

10 May, *Cry for Myth*, 99.

grand picture, big story, founding narrative. In each case it is a starting place, an inclusive vision, for understanding the world, including ourselves as participants in it.

Two dominant worldviews prevail in our culture. On the one side is the view of self-defined individualism; on the other is the scientific worldview. Each has a hold on us. In the activities of our daily lives we participate in each. Our encounters with these myths are not just as spectators looking at them critically and from a distance. We are part of them; we are caught up in them, and we live in an environment that has been formed by them. But their contradictions confuse us.

When we think of ourselves through the lenses of science we are small, insignificant, and morally neutral. A speck in a timeless, limitless universe, pushed along and controlled by forces we cannot comprehend. This scientific view diminishes our awareness that we are responsible agents.

When we think of ourselves as self-defined individuals we are free and morally egocentric. The timeline of our interests begins a little before our birth and extends just a little beyond our death. We try to sooth our angst by sticking with the present. Love is reduced to self-love, and our relationships with others are contracts for mutual benefit to which we turn when we are driven by insatiable yearning for things that we think will make us happy. They seldom do.

Both of these contemporary worldviews leave us with a spiritual vacuum or, as Rollo May says, hanging in mid-air. They do not allow us to understand ourselves as actors in a sacred and mysterious drama that we share with others who have lived before us, others who are living with us now, and others who will live on after we are gone. Without that way to place ourselves in a context of spiritual meaning, we find ourselves in a vacuum. We are reminded of the lyrics in Paul Simon's 1967 hit, "America": "I'm empty and aching and I don't know why."

TAKING OUR INVENTORY

If we pause and reflect on what Boomers have accomplished in forty years of our adulthood, it appears that we have both gained and lost. We now have:

- Astounding technology.
- An accelerating information culture that has global resources and global reach.

- A flexible view of truth.

- An expanded sense of personal license.

- Loss of community and personal alienation.

- A spiritual vacuum.

A look at the inventory gives us hints about why we feel tangled in freedom, about why our generation is glum. Are we stuck with what we have created? Is there anything we can do?

PART TWO

Rethinking Freedom, Reclaiming Virtue, and Searching for Meaning

8

Daring to Face the Truth about Ourselves

> Highest is truth, but higher still is truthful action.
>
> —Confucius[1]

BOOMERS HAD A HARD time growing up because they did not want to judge their own actions and admit what made some of them worthy and others not. Instead of asking if the way they lived made the world immediately around them any better, they turned their attention to getting the benefits they could garner from their new claims to freedom.

Nonchalant Boomers cultivated skepticism about religious faith and laughed along with Monty Python about the meaning of life. Many thought there was no point in joining with others to muse about life's big questions because they could come up with answers for themselves. Posters that said "The Meaning of Life: Whatever You Want It To Be" had a certain appeal. Clever quotes from Woody Allen were used to offset probing questions. Meanwhile many experienced that there were fewer ways to celebrate the mysterious and holy with others, because critics were quick to step forward and question whether there is anything we can ultimately count on to be meaningful.

On a more immediate plane many Boomers found it difficult to talk about good and evil because they had begun to doubt that the concepts had merit. Of the things that philosophers try to capture in words, few are

1. Confucius, *The Analects*.

as difficult to grasp as their ideas about what is good. The mere mention of good often starts debate. Who's good? Who gets to decide? Why should what you think is good be any better than what I think is good? What about the right we each have to our own opinions?

These questions reflect the difficulties encountered by those who try to give clear answers, but we do well to remember that knowing everything about good and knowing nothing are not the only possibilities. That we cannot agree on all points does not imply that all we know of good is random, subjective, or purely personal.[2] If we intend to tell the story of our own lives honestly, we must acknowledge that in our freedom we are able to choose for good or for ill. Our judgments matter, our intentions make a difference, and so do our actions.

When asked what they think of evil, many people reach for a story. They will remind you of what Hitler did, or some venal act committed in their community, or some dreadful thing that was done to them personally. Ask them to define good, and they will tell you about a neighbor who entered a burning house to save a child, or someone who donated a kidney to save a stranger. Seldom will they be able to give you a working definition of good, but that does not mean they are not able to recognize it. We know much about what is good and what is not from living with both good and evil.

Many metaphors that refer to good suggest it is a matter of the heart. We associate good with love: holding someone in our hearts, being joined heart to heart, or feeling that our hearts are full. We link it with courage when we take heart, put our whole hearts into something, and do not lose heart. We make promises from the bottom of our hearts and place our hands over our hearts to honor what we value deeply. We know that having a kind heart, a heart of gold, a soft heart, a tender heart, a big heart, or a pure heart is a sharp contrast to being heartless or cold-hearted. Much of what we understand about good is vital knowing. It is neither philosophical nor abstract. It is learned through experience.[3]

We may bicker about what notions of goodness are legitimate, but the simple fact of experience is that we have them. For example, we understand what it means to be the object of someone's ill will or indifference, just as

2. Scanlon, *What We Owe To Each Other*. Nagel, *The View from Nowhere*. Rorty, *The Identities of Persons*. Williams, "Persons, Character, and Morality." Kupperman, *Character*.

3. Herman, *Moral Literacy*.

we recognize when we are the recipients of kindness and good will. Most of us know something of each firsthand. Making judgments about our own behavior is more difficult because our reasons are woven together with our actions. Sometimes our convictions lead to our actions; those are the occasions we are quite sure we choose to act in a certain way because we are acting on principle. Just as often the opposite is true. Our convictions are formulated after the fact and motivated by the need to explain our actions.[4] Regardless of whether our explanations come before or after our actions, our explanations for why we behave as we do point to our belief that making right choices matters.

Most of us can admit that we ourselves have acted in ways that are good, and that we have also acted in ways that are not; however, we are inclined to call the latter our mistakes. Carol Tavris and Elliot Aronson are psychological researchers who have pulled together an extensive review of the many small steps we take to get our self-perception back in balance when we make mistakes. They demonstrate in their book, *Mistakes were Made (But Not by Me)*, how self-justifications interfere with our ability to be realistic about ourselves, making it easier to identify the mistakes made by others than it is to admit our own.

Our determination to be innocent puts us out of touch with evidence all around us, and the higher the stakes the more prone we are to these distortions. The thought and behavior patterns Tavris and Aronson expose are the ones we all use.[5] We want to believe that mistakes leading to negative outcomes are out of character for us; at the bottom line we want to be able to conclude that we are good. Assumptions about our own goodness are even more complicated when they are tangled up with the conviction that we are free, especially if that means that we should be free of guilt or shame for our own misdeeds as well as free of the judgment of others.

THE DENIAL OF EVIL

As they were reacting against the standards of the past and the expectations of their parents, many Boomers endorsed the idea that we are naturally good individuals who do negative things only when our reactions

4. Haidt, "The Emotional Dog and its Rational Tail: A Social Intuitionist Approach to Moral Judgment." Hauser, *Moral Minds: How Nature Designed Our Universal Sense of Right and Wrong*.

5. Tavris and Aronson, *Mistakes Were Made (But Not by Me)*.

are triggered by assaults upon our dignity and rights. Freeing up our true nature allows us to be better persons than our repressed ancestors were. In this atmosphere of unquestioned self-regard it is uncomfortable to talk about virtue, good and bad behavior, or responsibility for the well-being of others. Boomers wanted to believe in themselves without doubt, remorse, or regret.

When we appeal to freedom as a justification for our actions we often fail to consider several significant factors. First, some free actions are destructive. Boomers blame society for bad trends or blame "the system" for being destructive, but rarely are they willing to consider how they themselves, individually, are responsible for choices that cause suffering for others and themselves. In an age of unquestioned freedom, guilt is dismissed as neurotic and unhealthy. Self-criticism is a character weakness. We turn to therapists to help us escape our guilt and shame not by making amends for the harm we have done, but rather by interpreting circumstances to make the guilt or shame unreasonable or unnecessary.

Ask freethinking Boomers about evil, and they will tell you about someone else's bad behavior. Confront them about something negative in which they themselves have participated, and they hide behind the claim of free opinions. They insist that there are various points of view, and values are relative. They have little to say about what motivated their own mistakes other than to admit that if given the choice again they might exercise their freedom differently. The implication is that they have arrived at a different opinion about what they would do, but not necessarily that they have seen the error of their previous judgment.

Most of us want to believe that if we were in an unruly crowd stirred up for violence and looking for victims, we would stand aside and refuse to participate. We don't want to think that we could commit genocide, cheer on an executioner, or join with curious spectators at a lynching. When television news showed images of United States military personnel abusing prisoners at Abu Ghraib in Iraq, we were shocked. We wanted to believe that we are nothing like the monsters and misfits who do such things.[6] It was unsettling to discover that some of those abusers came from communities and families like our own. They are ordinary people like us.

In 1961 social philosopher Hannah Arendt was an observer in Jerusalem at the trial of Adolf Eichmann, a Nazi war criminal. She described

---

6. Zimbardo, *A Situationist Perspective on the Psychology of Evil: Understanding How Good People Are Transformed Into Perpetrators.*

him as "terrifyingly normal." He was not a raging sadist. He was shallow, banal, and indifferent to his victims. A thoughtless, mindless person. We have been reminded of this again more recently with the release of photos taken in the 1940s showing death camp guards celebrating holidays with their wives and girlfriends. The group is fresh-faced and happy. It is hard to imagine that on the job these same men were committing the grossest crimes against humanity.[7]

Lest we quickly put distance between villains and ourselves, we would do well to look back on the history of our own generation to see that we have not proved our innocence. It does not appear that freedom has made us better. Our generation has its full share of destruction, cruelty, and hate. Politicians have stooped to corruption, parents have damaged their children, lovers have abandoned each other, citizens have done injustice to their neighbors through bigotry or prejudice, business owners have cheated their customers and mistreated employees, and employees have done careless work that endangered the health and safety of others. In most cases the people who do these things feel free to act as they do and not give it a second thought. They are ordinary people who refuse to think beyond themselves.[8] It is not their evil intention that condemns them; it is that they do not care.

A second factor that shapes our judgments of what is and is not acceptable behavior is the presence of others. We seldom make our judgments in isolation. We form our own conclusions in the context of a powerful *folk psychology*, a set of assumptions we ourselves make about *what most people think*. It exerts pressure on what we judge to be natural and normal. While judging our own actions we are at the same time guessing how others, in general, would judge us. Furthermore these pressures are not isolated in moments here or there; they are continuous influences that shape our attitudes and predispositions gradually over time. We are not fully aware of the process of formation as it is occurring, but it is shaping us nonetheless.

The folk psychology that shapes us is hard to define. We cannot ascribe it to one source, authorities with names and faces, or significant mind-changing events. It is more complex than that. So instead we refer to it with more elusive terms like *culture*, our *social ethos*, or terms like *Boomer generation*. Even if it is vague, we intuit it. Metaphorically we might say it is

---

7. *Der Spiegel*, "Laughing at Auschwitz."

8 Arendt, *Eichmann in Jerusalem: A Report on the Banality of Evil* and *The Human Condition.*

in the air we breathe. It takes its shape in our own thinking in the form of what we assume other people, in general, are like.

Sometimes it is easier to grasp the power of social trends when we step back and look at the phenomenon from a distance. For example, we see it when we examine how television viewers of the 1950s were pressed to conclude that everyone else was like the nice families they watched on TV. Or we catch a moment of it when we recall that in the 1950s it was considered normal, if not cute, for children to dress up like cowboys and wear a holster with toy handguns. It is harder to focus the ways in which the ethos of culture shapes us in the present. There are moments, however, when we feel it pressing in on us and altering our judgment. This is especially so when we feel pushed to accommodate our behavior to new trends or social codes about which we are uncertain.

The third factor is closely related to the second. In order to have a platform from which to consider the larger culture around us we depend on the support of smaller communities within it. Rarely are we able to step back alone, one person at a time, and form our judgments of all the things that have changed in a generation. We are not entirely independent when we make judgments about whether the changes are for the better or whether the new behavior patterns are healthy and good. This also applies to our judgments about the habits and fashions formed by our changing convictions with regard to freedom.

In the long run it is important that we ask if those things we value most can be sustained as we absorb new attitudes about unrestrained freedom. If we have no community to hold us accountable, the risk of behaving mindlessly increases. We need a circle of persons to help us consider what is good beyond the range of personal interest. Its perspective is larger than the self-referential cloister of impulsive behavior or confident egocentrism. Its perspective is more disciplined than the amorphous and often grandiose pool of common assumptions that everyone supposedly knows is true. In order to know the full meaning of our actions we need to see them from the perspective of those who feel the impact of them, because we cannot see ourselves without a mirror. The honest presence of others helps us to challenge our own thinking.

It is helpful to distinguish the function of pressures that come from culture at large and the smaller scale influence of communities within it. Rarely are ordinary people able to engage the culture at large in any way that resembles dialogue. Public figures have platforms that allow them to address millions of people, but those who hear their assertions have no way to interact with the speaker. Listeners are passive spectators and have no avenues for response. By contrast, in communities of more immediate relationships it is possible to identify the pressures of the culture at large, and within the circle of a smaller community engage hearty dialogue about willingness or resistance to being formed by these influences. Within a fellowship of others who serve as our witnesses we can take responsibility for our choices.

It takes courage to admit to ourselves the patterns in our habits and the spots in our own lives at which we could live better if we made better choices. Doing this requires being conscious of the pressures on us, and being deliberate as we act in response to them. Why wouldn't we challenge ourselves this way? And that is a crucial question. Why don't we?

Among the messages from our culture at large are those encouraging us not to let others tell us what to do. We are pressured to be non-conformists, and oddly the pressure to conform to that standard of independence is very great. In short, we are confused and untrusting. In the Boomer generation while we were letting ourselves be persuaded that doing what we wanted and not letting others tell us what to do was a step of progress, we also developed habits of not seeing and not caring about matters for which we did not want to be responsible. Those habits shrunk our awareness. The space in which we think that what we do makes a difference has constricted, and the regions of our lives in which we feel helpless have expanded. Is this what we wanted?

By contrast to the pursuit of freedom that marked the Boomer generation, a more mature embrace of freedom requires recognizing that the freer we are the more responsible we also are. In an age of great license the limits are not being set for us. We are like drivers on a road without guardrails. We are frustrated if no one is taking responsibility for us, and we think they should. Meanwhile we are very skittish about accepting responsibility for ourselves.

Denying our responsibility to do what is good and right, whenever and wherever we can, ultimately degrades our self-esteem because denial distorts our perception of real circumstances and real consequences. We do this when we refuse to grow up, when we resist taking our own inventory, and when we close off feedback from others. We do this when we pretend that freedom justifies the blind pursuit of whatever strikes our fancy.

DOES VIRTUE MAKE ANY DIFFERENCE?

Some time ago in a conversation with a bright young woman I broached the matter of values. She told me she thinks of values as "the things that are important to you." When I asked her for an example she suggested that if someone is very concerned about eating right and staying healthy that would be one of their values. This young woman is conscientious about recycling and she frequently rides her bike instead of driving her car because she is concerned about fossil fuels and greenhouse gases. She would say these choices reflect her values.

I also asked my friend what she thinks about virtue. She smiled and admitted she thinks virtues are old-fashioned. The word tripped her up. It reminded her of a time when values had more to do with what other people thought of us. Back then a virtuous man worked hard and supported his family. A virtuous woman kept an orderly household and was faithful to her man. In the mind of my friend *virtue* was a word that was used before people figured out that what they do is their own business and that we all should be free to do what fits our own preferences.

We lost something when we downgraded our respect for virtues and set them aside as stuffy old rules. We lost a vocabulary for discussing what is good beyond individual preferences, personal tastes, and the ecstasy of pushing the limits of freedom. We now have a hard time sharing thoughts about what is good and being honest about what is not because the mention of these things is awkward. In short, we are intimidated by being perceived as judgmental. We are easily shamed when accused of being uptight, or old-fashioned, or narrow-minded.

Respect for virtue goes beyond the liberty to choose our own values. In the communal practice of virtue we tune ourselves to see how our actions contribute to good outcomes also for others, and how they may lead to misery for others as well. Experience viewed through the lens of virtue and tempered by the conscience of a vigorously self-assessing community restrains our sense of entitlement to do as we please in our own interests or for our own enjoyment. If we are willing to do this many times over and in many different circumstances, the attitudes of virtue become both flexible and durable dispositions. Overcoming our indifference allows us to align ourselves with what we believe makes the world better, and giving of ourselves for this purpose makes our lives more meaningful.[9] It is meaning not pleasure that is the reward of virtue.

When life does not roll out in sync with our values, even when we are in conflict with each other, we still have the choice to see good through the lens of virtue. The determination to see good is only altered by circumstances if we let it be. Doing this does not require that we ignore suffering or pretend that everyone and everything is lovely. It is not Pollyanna thinking. Virtue has a place in the presence of ugliness even when it has resulted from our own mistakes or after we have done things that we cannot change. Seeing good through the lens of virtue sustains our resolve to do the best we can in a world that is not ideal and with people, including ourselves, who are not always at their best.

Forty years into our experiment with freedom, it is becoming clear that unconsidered freedom that is indifferent to good is as likely to make us miserable as it is to make us happy. Opportunities embraced; opportunities wasted. Relationships deepened; relationships stunted. Health preserved; health squandered. Self-respect valued; self-respect shattered. We may no longer believe that the punishment for wrong is a snake pit in hell endured for eternity, but virtue does help us to see that how we think and what we do matters. Lest the mention of good and virtue set off panic about a return to authoritarianism, it is important to set out immediately that virtue is not a set of rigid rules. It is a constellation of attitudes oriented to discovering meaning in the way we live together.

As the stance of virtue becomes a disposition from which we watch what is happening around us, we become more accountable for how we live in many places:

1. Intimately as we share our lives with families and with friends.

2. Socially as we live together in neighborhoods, towns, states, or countries.

3. Vocationally as we learn how to produce and provide for others and ourselves.

4. Educationally as we extend what we know and share what we learn with others.

5. Culturally as we watch cinema, surf the 'net, read, and communicate with others.

9. Taylor, *Sources of the Self*, 47.

6. Environmentally as we realize that our habits impact mother earth.

7. Globally as we soften national aggression and recognize our interdependence.

8. Spiritually as we live in a world that existed before us and will go on after us.

It is a rare person who can think deeply about all these matters. It is also unclear what can be accomplished by musing about them in isolation. We need persons who can explore these things with open minds and spirits, committed to righteousness, so that they are able to offer fresh insight and wise guidance. Just as much we need a witnessing community that takes up what is offered and puts it to the test of life lived together, with commitment to do what is right and good. In short we need each other for the venture; we need a developed and dynamic community in order to grow in these ways together.

And so we must ask what makes us fit for community? What are the habits we might cultivate in ourselves to ready us for fellowship? Could it be that by shaping those attitudes in ourselves we would strengthen the fellowship we enjoy with others? Might it be then that our mindful participation would also sustain our courage to test the currents and speak the truth to each other, not driven by our determined freedom but by our commitment to seek what is good?

It seems reasonable to begin with the virtues that became devalued when we turned against being other-directed and turned toward being more boldly focused on ourselves. We cannot go back to the life we had before we became entangled in our freedoms. That time is no more. The world has changed. But we can revive our interest in those concerns that we set aside as if they were of little consequence. The place to begin is with our own personal inventory and with an examination of simple virtues.

Deepening our understanding of virtue is a spiritual practice. It coaxes us out of the cloister of self-focused individualism. Part Two of this book is a set of reflections that point a way toward reclaiming virtues we have displaced. When the discussion here suggests *we* have displaced them it is not meant to imply that every individual has given up concern with doing good. On the contrary, there are many individuals who daily work to be positive influences, they determine to live morally, they want to do right in their dealings with others. Despite this we live in a cultural atmosphere that bombards us with messages suggesting that others do not care. Too often we find ourselves in the predicament of thinking that if we care about good we stand alone because others are free do as they please, and they do so with indifference.

There is psychological evidence to suggest that our own self-protectiveness orients us to notice negative events. Maybe we neglect noticing good because we are anxious and feel threatened. That might explain why bad behavior is more newsworthy than good behavior, but it is not a reason to conclude that there are more bad things happening than good. Even though there are voices from many different places warning us that we live in a disillusioned culture and in a directionless time, it is worth noticing that the warnings usually come from those who wish it were not so.

In our gloomiest moments we may feel pressured by forces all around us to accept that we live in a lousy world. If we allow ourselves to be convinced by that we may stop seeing good. We may fall into a self-defeating pattern of finding company only in the gathering of fellow complainers. The fellowship of negativity is a dangerous form of banality, and it is no wonder if it leaves us feeling gloomy. And more than that if we stop seeing good we may become dispirited so that we stop believing there is any point to doing good. In this bleak place our fellowship with others will have no growing edge, no surge of hope, no trust in the future. It will be sterile and unproductive. The alternative is to reclaim virtue. To bring back into our habits those attitudes and dispositions that allow us to see good more clearly because we are looking for it, and then to join together with others to advance the good whenever and however we can.

Virtues, as we will explore them here, are not rules for behavior. They do not dictate our actions. Virtues are habits of watching. Seeing good through the lenses of virtue brings us back to the awareness that our own actions matter. Each time we see good more clearly there are more reasons to choose for good if we can. Virtues coach us in the discovery of meaning. They encourage us as we embrace freedom with responsibility, and they clarify our intentions so we can resist becoming entangled in the narcissism that so easily grows out of unconsidered freedom.

9

Gratitude Makes a Difference

If we want to make the most out of opportunities to flex our gratitude muscles,
then we must creatively look for new
situations and circumstances in which to be grateful.

—Robert Emmons[1]

WHEN I WAS A child I was told a story of two brothers who were each given the seedling for a prized apple tree. They planted the trees, watered them, protected them from bugs, and watched the trees grow. Eventually the trees bloomed, and then the fruit appeared. The one boy was so eager for the apples that as soon as they were the size of little golf balls he picked them all and ate them. His reward was a terrible stomach ache. The other brother waited until the apples had ripened. Not only did he enjoy the delicious fruit, but also he had enough apples to sell at the roadside. He was generously rewarded for his effort and his patience. The point of telling a story like this to children was to teach them not to be impatient and greedy like the boy with the stomach ache.

Adults wanted children to learn the benefits of *delayed gratification*.[2] They encouraged children to sell cookies and chocolate door to door in

1. Emmons, *Thanks*, 206.

2. Goleman, *Emotional Intelligence*, 80-83. Metcalfe and Mischel, "A Hot/Cool-System Analysis of Delay of Gratification: Dynamics of Willpower." Funder et al., "Delay of Gratification; Some Longitudinal Personality Correlates."

order to earn their way to camp. It was expected that children would stand in line patiently at the amusement park because to get on the best rides they had to put forth the effort of waiting. Adults who encouraged children to do these things were eager to tell them that first comes effort and patience and only later the reward. That was the order of events in lessons meant to develop character.

Baby Boomers growing older are reflecting back on the past, and they see a stark contrast between the lives of their parents and the lives of their children. They remember fathers and mothers who tirelessly supported the family by working two or three jobs to make ends meet. They often set aside their own comforts, and many never got to cash in on delayed rewards. There were families who were miserably poor; men and women whose hardscrabble lives broke their spirits. There were also many who scraped by day-to-day and week-to-week but they never got ahead.

Even those who appeared to prosper were sometimes broken by the price they paid for their success. Pursuit of the American dream was hard work. It was not like winning the lottery. The story is told that when Arthur Miller's *Death of a Salesman* first played on stage the audiences wept. Miller's friend Elia Kazan recalls hearing "men sob in the theater." He recollects that, "Night after night, I would stand there and you would hear these resonant, deep voices, expressing their pain."[3]

Sometimes the rise from poverty corrupted the souls of those ambitious enough to persist, and they took the detour through the dark side. In *The Winter of Our Discontent* John Steinbeck portrays his character, Ethan Hawke, who struggles his way out of the shame of poverty and leaves an escape route littered with victims. He is a man whose burden of failure becomes a burden of guilt.[4] Despite our inclination to idealize the worn survivors of the past, the life of the Greatest Generation was often difficult, and not all of them were heroes. Boomers may admire their parents for their grit, but they would not want to live their lives. We expect life to be better than that.

The goals of the Greatest Generation were built on fear of failure and the pursuit of security. The motives of the Boomer Generation and their children are based on pursuit of that to which they feel entitled. Much has changed, but there are two common themes that have appeared over and over again in our culture's attitudes about "the good life."

3. Gottfried, *Arthur Miller: His Life and Work*, 149.
4. Steinbeck, *The Winter of Our Discontent*.

> Be Happy—get something you want.
> Don't Be Satisfied—there is always more you deserve.

These messages clatter around in our psyches creating a chaos of desire. Happy one moment, we are wanting again the next. We are not able to settle down into a stable state of contentment in which we are satisfied and grateful. We may be fearful of satisfaction if it causes us to doubt that we will ever get what we want. Once satisfied we might not know what to do next, and the satisfied life could be a flatline. If that is the way we think, we will keep projecting our wants and pursuing them.

Despite the similarities from one generation to the next, there is also something that has changed in our expectations. In forty years of adulthood Boomers have turned the scheme for delayed gratification upside down. What began as a reaction to their parents has now been carried forward as an attitude prevalent among their children. Boomers feel more entitled to what they want than their parents did. As adults Boomers and their children believe they deserve to have their wishes come true, and they deserve to be happy. They no longer bother with patience. They are likely to help themselves to what they think they deserve and be disgruntled if something stands in their way. If life does not pan out that way, they take it as a personal injury, proof that life is unfair.

This way of thinking shaped behavior in a credit economy. We are open to messages assuring us that certain kinds of happiness are priceless, and it is okay to charge them to a credit card. Having now and paying later is the way millions handle finances. Meanwhile lessons of delayed gratification are forgotten. Not only have we scaled down the value of patience, we have also come to think that frustration is a bad thing. We may tolerate some stress in our own lives, but we go to great lengths to spare our children.

We are cautious about putting too much pressure on children by expecting them to work for what they want. The possibilities of success that are placed before young people are often those not requiring effort or discipline. Instead we encourage young people to be free-spirited and creative; whatever the result, we affirm them for it. We feel obligated to provide our children with the things they claim they need. Furthermore it is not hard to convince us that if something would be good to do, it is better to do it sooner than later. That is why few parents of college students dare to tell their sons and daughters that the costly semesters abroad they are planning may be something they could save for and do later, because they will appreciate the experience more if they fund it themselves.

These patterns are not true of every individual, but they are active in the atmosphere of our culture. We feel the pressure. Increasingly the accumulation of rewards is the way our culture judges an individual's worth. Those who have wealth are honored for it; those who lack it are humbled by it. We speak of personal worth in terms of the dollar value of an individual's assets. Lists publish the names of the wealthiest people in the world, and being on them is a badge of honor. Life is going well if we are feeling good often enough, and the rich are lucky, we assume, because they have the means for buying things that make them feel good.

Pleasure and contentment are easily confused. In a prosperous economy it is far easier to be well-informed about the full range of rewards than it is to be clear about the way of contentment. Despite the abundance of rewards, satisfaction is out of reach if we keep absorbing mixed messages about what we should want next. If we train ourselves to think that no matter how much we have, we need something more or something better, contentment will elude us. We can identify moments of pleasure, but they are fleeting. We can identify possessions that appeal to us, but often not having them holds more power over us than what we derive from finally acquiring them. Delayed gratification has been displaced by our belief that *immediate gratification* is better.

One of the ways that our pursuit of gratification differs from our parents' is the reversal of effort and reward. Our effort phase often begins after we get what we want or after we have already consumed what we purchased on credit. The pleasure of acquisition is already past, the exciting time is already over, and we still have to put forth the effort to earn it. The size of the national debt in the United States is a stunning reminder of how habituated we have become to spending first and paying later or never paying at all.

As a result of reversing effort and reward, the work we do in order to pay our way is more like the chore of cleaning up the trash after a party. Someone has to take care of it, but the goal is to get rid of it. Who would look at the trash after a party and say: "Oh how lovely; it must have been a very nice party." Who looks at the credit card statement after a vacation and says: "It was such a nice vacation; I will enjoy working now to pay for it."

Once we have consumed the things, adventures, or services we purchase, we are less interested in the means to achieving them. The effort and the reward are disconnected. The effort and the dignity are disconnected too. By the time we feel the obligation to pay, we are often on our way to pursuing the next pleasure. Rather than being a motivator debt is a burden. The leftover efforts required to pay for past events are an inconvenience, a lingering and unpleasant side effect of our enjoyment. Something we would be happy to forget if we could, but we can't. They remain there as reminders that we are behind in our pursuit of gratification. Somewhere in this sequence a step has been lost. We do not know when to be grateful. In the reversal of effort and reward it always seems either too early or too late.

Why do we live this way? Are we less strong than our parents and unable to resist the temptation of indulgence? Did we fail to absorb the storybook lessons of childhood? Do we have less ability to understand consequences? I suspect that the reason is quite simple. We live this way because we can. Structures have been created that allow us to operate this way, and they have been created for us by others who benefit every time we use them. Our parents did not live the way we do because they could not. The opportunities were not available to them.

There is another factor, however, that may be equally important in understanding the shift from our parents' generation to ours. We live this way because *we have displaced the virtue of gratitude and have put in its place a sense of entitlement.* It is one of the ways we are entangled in freedom, and it is reinforced in a culture of narcissism.

THE HABITS OF OUR DISCONTENT

Many years ago, long before I was a parent myself, I babysat for a family whose children were, in simple terms, spoiled. One evening while we were waiting for their mother to finish getting ready to go out, I sat in the kitchen chatting with their dad. He commented to me that he and his wife were delighted that I continued to watch their children because they had experienced burnout with some of their previous sitters. The father of my charges was a man of good humor, and he chuckled when he told me that what their family needed was someone like Mary Poppins who could straighten the kids out. "They are good kids," he said, "but they are little gods of the moment. They want what they want, and they want it now."

There is another chapter to the story of these little gods of the moment. It is the story of their father. He was a man who had pulled himself up by his own bootstraps. He had become affluent; the reputation that floated around was that he had a Midas touch. It may have been that he stepped into the right business at just the right time, but in the case of this man he personally took credit for his success. The children of this successful man were extensions of him. They were little gods of the moment; he was a big god of an ample lifestyle. He spent his life in pursuit of what he thought would make him happy. Among the things he seemed to believe would make him happy were money and happy children.

The children often acted as if getting what they wanted would make them happy, and they demonstrated this by being very unhappy and miserable if their desires were thwarted. They had found their father's weakness. In most of his life this man was immune to fear, but he was intimidated by the mere suggestion that his children were unhappy. He had to keep them happy. He could not deny them the pleasures they demanded, at least if they were pleasures that money could buy. In this respect he was consistent. He was generous with himself and equally generous with his family.

There was only a minor difference between the father and the children in that he had learned that sometimes you have to be patient before you cash in grandly. He knew about delayed rewards. I am not sure he knew about satisfaction, but he did know not to pluck the apple before it was ripe. By contrast the other members of his family were high maintenance consumers. They demanded their rewards immediately. What I do not remember about this family was that it was happy.

Both the adults and the children were often disgruntled. The missing element in this family picture was gratitude. Even when their demands were met they were not impressed for long, because they had to keep proving their worth with yet another test of whether or not they could have what they wanted. It seems they could not see a reason to be grateful when what they received was nothing more than that to which they had a right.

If we assume that what we already have does not merit gratitude, we enter a chronic state of discontentment. The habits of discontentment let us believe that until we have all that we want we do not have what we deserve. We delay gratitude and set up conditions for happiness that are impossible to fill. Even if rewards are attainable, the satisfaction is not attainable because we keep moving the finish line. The right time for gratitude never comes.

- The millionaire says I will be satisfied when I have made a cool billion.

- The car buff says I will be pleased when I get the new model.

- The bachelor says I will be happy when I find the perfect lover.

- The student says I will be more motivated after I graduate and get a job.

- The worker says I will be content after I retire and can play.

If we are motivated by a perennial state of want and restlessness, nothing is ever enough. Because we cannot see the good in the present, we are locked into a state of poverty no matter how much money we have, a state of disappointment no matter how many things we get, a state of loneliness no matter how perfect our partner, a state of restlessness no matter what our opportunities, and a state of boredom no matter how much we play.

Gratitude does not lull us into being content with less than we need, but greed can seduce us into thinking that we need everything we want because it impairs our ability to distinguish what we want from what we need. Distinguishing need and want are not as difficult as we might think. We can sort them out by looking at the consequences of deficiency. When we do not have what we need, bad things happen. The hiker who lacks water in the desert may die of dehydration. The patient who cannot acquire the antibiotic to stop an infection may lose a limb or life.

Not having what we want has different consequences. If I do not get the new car I have had an eye on, or if I cannot go on the vacation that I have been waiting for, what difference will it really make? I have some choices. I might let go of my wish and recognize that now is not the time for filling this want. If I accept real circumstances my want disappears. If greed and desire blind me to my limits, however, I may think getting what I want is a measure of my worth. Greed plays terrible tricks with the mind. It can persuade us that life is unfair and we have been cheated. Unfilled wants are a choice, and if not having what we want makes us miserable, it is a punishment we inflict upon ourselves.

THE GRATITUDE CYCLE

In addition to the discontent we feel if we cannot distinguish what we want from what we need, we suffer another loss. Greed and discontentment isolate us because they take us out of the cycle of gratitude and generosity. When I feel sorry for myself I do not see my part as a contributor to the ongoing flow of good that we all share. If I think I have nothing to give because I owe no one anything, I am locked in a lonely state of poverty no matter how much I have.

Gratitude has little to do with the rewards we get. Of course it is very lovely if we are grateful because something extraordinarily good has happened; however, gratitude is also a habit, an attitude, a state of mind. It has much to do with seeing the good wherever and whenever it becomes apparent. Gratitude is one of the frames of reference through which we perceive blessing in our own lives. If we believe that good is worth celebrating, gratitude is a stance from which we are more likely to see it. It helps us notice.[5]

While delaying pleasure is not a bad thing, delaying gratitude is a risk. If we neglect to see good because we are pursuing rewards for later, we delay gratitude and break the habit. We may be recipients of generosity and refuse to know it because we are accustomed to taking it for granted. Entrenched in the habits of delayed gratitude, we may be consumed with a getting phase that never ends so that the point of contentment is never reached. Putting off gratitude, displacing it, may leave us chronically restless and dissatisfied.

As children we learned the etiquette of gratitude by saying "please" and "thank you," but we did not necessarily learn their meaning. Saying "please" involves a contract between two people when something good is about to happen. It sets up the attitude before the action starts. *Please* is a promise of sorts; the promise is to be gratified (pleased). It establishes that the exchange that is about to take place is one of good will, and that it is meant to be agreeable to both parties. *Please* is not the last word. When the deed is done we also say "thank you." That is another kind of contract.

The word *thank* comes from the same root in English as the word *think*.[6] When we say "thank you" we are acknowledging that we have noticed another's kindness. We are making a commitment to be mindful that something good has happened, to give thought to it. *Please* is an attitude we put in place before the action starts, and *thank you* is an attitude we put in place after the action is completed. These little words bracket the exchange with good intentions.

When we were children saying "please" was hard to remember sometimes, and "thank you" sometimes took effort. That is why when we were on our way out the door and headed to someone else's house our mothers would remind us to watch our manners. For an enthusiastic kid there were

5. There is a strong link between gratitude and general life satisfaction, and also between gratitude and positive behavior toward others. McCullough et al., "The Grateful Disposition: A Conceptual and Empirical Topography." McCullough et al., "Is Gratitude a Moral Affect?" Seligman et al., "Positive Psychology Progress." Emmons, *Thanks*.

6. *The Oxford English Dictionary*.

things more interesting than watching manners. Similarly writing thank you notes or making a call to someone to acknowledge a gift was a chore. Acting like an adult when you are a child can be hard work. As adults we become proficient at *please* and *thank you* so that we can toss them out with hardly a second thought. We do not have to mind our manners because they are automatic. They are mindless habits. Unfortunately we may be no more conscious now than we were as children of the many ways in which life is good to us, but we are smoother.

This morning I had to call tech support to get some help with my computer. I am sure I made the request politely with a *please*, and I probably ended the call with a *thank you*. Honestly, I don't remember that I did, but I am claiming I said these things because I would like to think that my manners are not getting rusty. That I am not becoming one of those people who cranks at anonymous customer service staff on the phone.

Sometimes it is not clear to me that *please* and *thank you* make much difference. I am not as mindful as I would like to be. What if I were more mindful? What if I pushed myself beyond my empty civility and really meant it when I said "please"? Just saying it might help me notice the effort of the anonymous person on the phone line even if she is miles away. I would be reminded that she has a job, and sometimes it must try her patience. It is not a job that I would like, so it would help me be aware that she does an unpleasant job with grace. Perhaps she also has a life, a family, something else she is dealing with today that is difficult. And still she is helpful. If I could be mindful of her efforts I could also genuinely mean it when I say "thank you" to her.

By making the effort to be grateful for simple goods, I might become more conscious of the efforts of others to be positive. And I might be happier because I would be more alert to the fact that the world is a more generous place than I recognize when I am indifferent to it. This is not to say that there are no moments in our lives that are deeply distressing and people whom we encounter who are downright nasty. But gratitude does not let these disagreeable moments have the last word. Gratitude brings us back to looking for good. The examples we are using here may seem trivial. That is the point. They are not exceptional. We never have to look far to see good.

Some of the obstacles that clutter our vision of good grew out of the ways we displaced gratitude while we were pursuing our own freedom. We had a hard time seeing good when we were in the business of changing the world by fighting against what is negative. It would have required maturity we did not have to be grateful to the parents who we thought had messed up the world we inherited. When we were raging against injustice we did not have the largesse to pause and be thankful for the good things that had come to us personally.

We were critics and revolutionaries; gratitude did not fit our mindset. Angry students on university campuses did not pause to say "thank you for the good education I am receiving" before putting graffiti on the wall or disrupting a campus meeting. When we were throwing out the past and looking for a future of our own making we did not pause to consider that we had benefitted from the legacies of the past. Gratitude slipped out of our generation's folk character; it was no longer part of the image that we formed of ordinary people. Along with our high standards regarding what was owed to us, we were the generation that ushered in an age of narcissism. It was one of the symptoms of our refusal to grow up, and it was fortified by our belief that it was within our power to redefine personal freedom and remain young forever.

Our stand against gratitude was apparent in our language and our actions. We were inclined to think that gratitude was servile. Beyond our assumption that we owed no one anything if we have been disappointed and they were at fault, we also came to believe that we owed no one anything because we were free. Whatever good came our way was not something we received out of the generosity of others; it was something to which we felt we were entitled. In our irritation with a society that disappointed us in significant ways, we were afraid that being grateful might be taken as an admission that there was no need for change, and that we were satisfied with everything just the way it was. We used our discontentment to make a point, and we withheld our gratitude to further reinforce our message.

The Boomer generation replaced gratitude with the pursuit of pleasure, but they are not the same thing. Unless we are willing to recognize that we receive from others, we easily confuse gratitude with things it is not:

- Gratitude is not a *payback*. It is not something that we give back in order to cancel out the effort that someone else has extended for us. Two goods do not cancel each other out. They are added to each other.

- Gratitude is not a *put-down*. If I am grateful to you it is not because in your generosity toward me you are now in a one-up position, and I am forced to admit it.

- Gratitude is not *indebtedness*. My gratitude to you for your kindness does not set me up to do something of equal value for you in the future. Admitting my gratitude is not the same as signing an IOU.

- Gratitude is not a form of *flattery*. It is not my way of saying to you that you are better than everyone else in this dreary world because you did something kind for me.

- Gratitude is not a form of *manipulation*. It is not my way of cheering you on when you are nice to me so that you will keep delivering the goods.

Gratitude, generosity, and contentment are all of one piece. When we are genuinely grateful it strengthens our sense that we enjoy the good in life because we are woven into the fabric of life with others. The energy of our gratitude transforms into generosity toward others. Ultimately when we participate in the ongoing cycle of loving-kindness, receiving with gratitude and giving generously, we find contentment.

GRATITUDE IS A DECISION

We may have missed occasions for gratitude because we were not paying attention. It is never too late to notice. We may have underestimated an act of kindness because we did not open our hearts to it. It is never too late to feel grateful. We may have stepped out of the cycle of gratitude and not communicated our pleasure and thankfulness, but it is never too late to express that we are grateful. And it is never too late to allow gratitude to flow through us into generosity because we have today to do it.

There are things we can do if we wish to shape our hearts to gratitude. We can remember today those things in the past for which we are grateful. We can look around and identify what is happening for which we are grateful today. We can say "please" and "thank you," and notice how we feel if we mean it. We might make a wish list and notice that even if those wishes do not come true we already are surrounded with plenty.

A few years ago someone gave me a bumper sticker that promoted random acts of kindness.[7] I did not put it on my bumper. I put it in a drawer. At first I wondered why the acts should be random. Aren't planned acts of

---

7. Random Acts of Kindness Foundation, *Practice Random Acts of Kindness: Bring More Peace, Love, and Compassion into the World.*

kindness just as good? Don't tax deductible contributions count? What is wrong with putting reminders on a calendar?

Gradually it occurred to me that deliberate acts of kindness are easier, because there are more reminders to do them. I send a birthday card to some people each year because the reminder is on my calendar. I send a little note commending my coworker for handling a meeting well today, and two weeks from now I will lead the meeting and count on my coworker for support. Routine acts of kindness get woven in with our habits, and we get used to them. They make sense and are good to do, even if they are not the blossom of spontaneous gratitude.

Random acts of kindness require a special sort of mindfulness. To perform a random act of kindness you have to be watching for an opportunity. A little light needs to go on in your awareness when the opportunity arises. This leads to a shift in your mindset. You are a different person when you go through your day looking for places in which your own random and small acts could bring a moment of kindness to the world. These small acts have potential to keep repeating themselves. They forge a new attitude.

Acts of kindness do not require that you set aside everything else you do in order to make kindness your project. You can go right on with your work. You can keep your schedule as always. These acts are not dramatic demonstrations of your goodness; they are small expressions of your mindset. They are a new frame of reference from which you are intending to see the good that is all around you.

The simple mindfulness of a *please* and *thank you* does have the power to open our hearts for a moment if we let it. A random act of kindness may change the world a little, but it can change us a lot. Gratitude enjoyed as an ongoing and continuous cycle of mindfulness leads away from greed and toward generosity. It feels good to be grateful. It also feels good to be generous. We feel heartened when we see and when we do good. The beauty of gratitude is that it is its own reward.

10

Offloading Anger

Anger is a weed; hate is the tree.

—AUGUSTINE[1]

I WAS WALKING IN the park and heard a child crying. It was not a cry of pain, panic, or fear. It was the distinct cry of protest. A loud, insistent, angry cry. When I looked at where the cry was coming from, I saw a little fellow in a total meltdown because the woman he was with, his mother or caretaker, was putting him back into his stroller. There was no mistaking it; he was not happy. Maybe he did not want to be strapped in, or maybe he just wanted to stay longer at the park.

The image of this angry child stayed with me as I continued my walk. I was impressed by how little he was and how strong and loud his complaint. From his size I could guess that he could not understand the conflict. He was too young. There was something he wanted, and his will was being thwarted. He was frustrated.

This experience brought to mind another event some years ago that taught me something about wrath, but this was not the anger of a child. Through my work I met a woman who is a "foodie." During our breaks we swapped recipes and shared thoughts about our favorite ethnic restaurants. As we became better acquainted she invited my husband and me to come to her home for dinner. She promised a great ethnic meal because she had

1. Augustine of Hippo, *Sermones*, 58.

learned from her mother-in-law to cook the recipes of her husband's family, and she was eager to share them with us. True to her promise the food was extraordinary.

If you are wondering what this has to do with anger that is the next part of the story. We met my friend's husband for the first time when we got together for the meal at their home. He was a warm and cordial host; his charm and his delightful sense of humor brightened the conversation. We sat around the table drinking coffee after dinner, and the conversation turned to the story of his family: his parents, grandparents, uncles, aunts, and cousins. He recounted the history of a large extended family of which only his mother and her two siblings had survived ethnic cleansing and genocide. The rest of the family had been wiped out.

Listening to our host I had an experience I have had often after meeting someone face to face for the first time. Never could I have guessed his story. So often we do not know the memories that live behind a face. As he continued telling us about his family, he became more personal and passionate. He told how he hated those people who had destroyed his family. He admitted that today if he met some of them in a forest and was sure no one would know about it, he could shoot them through the head and leave them to die. He said he could do this without any guilt. He would welcome the chance to do to them what they did to his family. As he told this dreadful story his face changed. Hard cold rage came over him.

Only later as we were driving home did it dawn on me that, given our host's age and when these events had happened, they had all occurred before his birth. He had not witnessed the events about which he told. He had never met the persons to whom it happened, but their story was his story nonetheless. The people he imagined executing in the woods were the children of those persons who had murdered his family. For him the images and feelings were as fresh as if he had been there and it had happened yesterday.

Anger seems natural in the case of the little boy in the park. He was a child frustrated because the good time was ending. We can assume that he got over it, and his disappointment will not be part of his enduring memory. It would be lovely to think that within the hour he was somewhere else, playing happily, and that the meltdown in the park had been erased. The anger of our dinner host is another matter. It goes much deeper than frustration. It is wrath. His injury is scored so deep into his memory, he may never get past it. He is living proof that the legacy of hate can be carried forward from generation to generation. A spontaneous conversation with new acquaintances at dinner triggered the recollection and stoked the rage all over again.

We do not have to reach far into our own imaginations to venture some guesses as to why my dinner host has held his rage so long. If he relinquishes his anger he may feel that he is betraying his relatives and forgetting their suffering. Dropping his fantasy of revenge may imply for him that he has accepted what happened. That he no longer objects to it. Were he to give up his rage he might feel disarmed, but he wants to believe that he could stand up and refuse to be a victim if he or his own young family were under attack. All of the fears that feed his anger are feelings we can understand because, were we standing in his place, we might hold tight to our anger too.

Would my friend be better off without his anger? Does it serve a clear purpose that is worth the misery it causes him? Does he need to remember so that he can hold his resolve to prevent such horrors from ever happening again? My friend's family must have suffered terribly, but he has also suffered because he carries the burden of anger turned to hate. Neither he nor his family chose to be victims. It was done to them. As the bearer of the memory he lives with the lingering consequences of someone else's act. It is his wound. He feels he has no choice about his anger. Even if my friend had the option to relinquish his anger, I suspect he would not want to give it up.

What can we conclude about anger? Is it natural and necessary? Can we shape and control our anger? Can we distinguish temporary frustration from enduring wrath? Does anger have anything to do with good, or is it the inevitable leftover of a bad experience?

IS ANGER NATURAL?

In 1988 the psychologist Paul Ekman released a summary of his cross-cultural studies of emotion. Over the course of nearly two decades he had visited cultures around the world where he studied emotion by measuring facial muscles, making photographs of facial expressions, and conducting interviews. On the basis of his work Ekman came to the conclusion that there are six emotions that are universal. Anger is one of them.[2]

Although anger is universal, the triggers for it and the tolerance for its expression are shaped by culture. In the 1950s many youngsters in the

2. Ekman and Davidson, *The Nature of Emotions.*

United States were taught that parents and other adults are authority figures with whom children should cooperate. If adults gave instructions, children were expected to comply. Many Baby Boomers were raised in families in which a child who resisted adult instruction might be told: "When you grow up you can do things your way, but for now you will do this my way." In these settings children had to learn to manage their anger because adults would not tolerate uncontrolled expressions of frustration if it demonstrated defiance.

During the 1960s attitudes toward child rearing in the United States went through a significant reversal. By the 1970s when Baby Boomers began raising their own children, the new generation of parents had been put on notice that they should not frustrate their children. Youth culture had unseated authority figures, and that included parents. Responsibility for the formation of children was still part of the parental agenda, but progressive parents believed that they could accomplish this with plenty of freedom and a little gentle coaxing. Furthermore they were told by experts that children should be free to express their negative feelings because suppressing them would cause damage.

If there were power struggles between parents and children, progressive parents were expected to tread lightly lest the child's creativity be stifled and its self-esteem injured. The parents whose generation had declared "Question Authority!" were now the authorities being questioned. Their own children were putting them to the test. We might have expected this as a generational progression, but there is one additional element that made this a dramatic reversal of roles: it became permissible to question authority, but not to question children. This fit well with the belief that the world belongs to the young.

In the free spirited atmosphere of the 1970s and 80s frustration was considered toxic, something to be gotten rid of as quickly as possible. It violated a child's worth and rights. Furthermore children growing up this way did not relinquish the permissiveness of childhood once they reached adulthood. They continued to assume that, with the possible exception of parents frustrated by children, no one should have to tolerate frustration. Small doses of frustration might not be harmful, but they should be mild and brief. If society's expectations were frustrating, then society needed to change.

In the 1950s if a child's behavior countered an authority figure's rules, the child felt guilty and the authority figure felt angry. By the 1970s if an authority figure frustrated children, the children felt angry and the authority figure was blamed. Society had reshaped its code for family life and extended it to society in general. We had come to assume that we deserve a life with minimum frustration, and that we should be free to have our natural desires satisfied. When it does not turn out that way we feel angry, and we feel free to express it.

RESPONSIBLE ANGER

Readiness for anger is a habit. A disposition. There is growing evidence that individuals have *set points* for anger. Some individuals have a high set point, and it takes a great deal to provoke them. Others have a low set point, and it takes very little to tip them over into an active angry state. As a result they are angry much of the time.

Clinical researchers refer to the level of continuous anger readiness as *trait anger*. This is in contrast to *state anger*, which is a reaction to a specific event. Trait anger is a feature of personality. It may be partly genetic or a function of how the brain is wired. It may also be related to other physical states including exposure to chemicals and drugs. Persons with high levels of trait anger are hyper alert to things that offend them. They are easily frustrated, primed to fight back when provoked, and quick to blame others for their own behavior. With so much practice exercising their anger, they become fluent in communicating it but inept at managing their anger to keep it from burning out of control.

Recently I was in a clothing store and paying for something at the counter. While the clerk was helping me, a woman who had a pair of jeans in her hand stepped up to ask the clerk for a different size. The clerk explained that all the items of that style had been put out in the store, and if the size she was looking for was not on the rack, it meant they did not have anymore. Apparently that was not what the customer wanted to hear because she threw down the jeans she was holding, muttered the F-word, and stomped out of the store.

Neither the clerk nor I paid much attention to the angry customer because this behavior, though unpleasant, is not so unusual as to be shocking. We rolled our eyes a little and went on with our transaction. Our culture tolerates the rude and insulting outbursts of frustrated people. It happens on the road, in public places, in the workplace, and in many households.

Our folk psychology pressures us to accept that the free expression of anger is natural.[3]

Is that all we can say? Anger is natural? Something like hiccups? Something we would rather not have if given a choice, but if we do have it, well then that is just the way it is.

HOW WE SHAPE OUR PREDISPOSITION FOR ANGER

Anger comes in different forms. We are frustrated when our pleasure and comfort are disrupted, especially if we judge the frustration to be unnecessary or unfair. When our safety and well-being are threatened, defensive anger pumps up our power to protect ourselves. We experience social anger when we take offense at someone's moral misdeed, or failure to meet an obligation.

Anger is also part of our cultural heritage, that big story that we weave together with our own personal story in composing the narrative of our lives. The 1960s has been called an angry era. The new generation coming into adulthood was angry enough to start a revolution, and we have continued to be angry about many things ever since. The cultural legacy that we are handing along to the generations that follow us is also laced with deep and pervasive hostilities.

Consider the shock waves of fear, grief, and rage that flooded through the United States after September 11, 2001. We had been the victims of violence, and we were sure that what was done was more than unfair. The sense of attack was felt by those who were at Ground Zero and equally by those who were miles away. The outrage caught on among those not personally acquainted with the individuals who were injured or who perished in the attacks. It felt as if we had all been attacked. On that day even mildly patriotic Americans were more consciously American than usual. It was a national moment, and it mobilized a communal sense of outrage.

Anger is contagious. When many people experience the same frustration at the same time it creates a reverberating shock wave. They check in with each other and watch how others handle their feelings. Gradually they get in stride with each other. Out of this experience comes a shared

3. DiGiuseppe and Trafrate, *Understanding Anger Disorders*. Spielberger et al., "Assessment of Anger: The State-Trait Anger Scale." Evces et al., "Effect of Trait Anger on Cognitive Processing of Emotional Stimili." Wilkowski and Robinson, "Guarding Against Hostile Thoughts; Trait Anger and the Recruitment of Cognitive Control."

story and new ways to communicate the gravity of the event. *Terrorist cells, Homeland Security, War on Terror, Al Qaeda, Weapons of Mass Destruction, Jihad, Radical Islam, Twin Towers, Ground Zero,* and *Axis of Evil* were added to the public vocabulary in the months following the disaster of September 2001. These words and the conversations in which they were embedded were laden with emotion, intense anger mingled with fear and sadness.

Collective anger is powerful. The angry stories of 9/11 converged on a common version, and it became increasingly difficult for anyone to question its elements. Attached to the common story was a test of patriotism, because questioning the story or its heroes was considered treacherous and unpatriotic. For example, when the President declared that the enemies of the United States did this to us because "they hate our freedoms," few dared to question his judgment. His use of these words was a sure way to stir the anger of freedom-loving Americans. Something sacred was under attack, and what is more sacred to us than our freedom? No one dared to ask if what the terrorists had done was in revenge for something that was done to them, or whether we understood their motives correctly. Not excusing them or agreeing with them, just hearing them accurately. Anger and the pressure to conform in the presence of angry people is a powerful controller. It silenced anyone who was inclined to question the President's interpretation of events.[4]

The way we formed our story together unleashed a series of responses that changed the landscape of the United States. Today we walk through security gates whenever we enter government facilities, go to large public gatherings, or are in groups that include high profile figures. Agencies track ingredients that could be used for homemade bombs. A misplaced package in a public place can escalate into an incident that requires vacating a building and disrupting the schedules of innocent people. Persons with swarthy complexions and dark hair must go out of their way not to appear suspicious. In order to conform to security procedures we allow agents to intrude on our privacy in ways that once would have been objectionable. We live in a post 9/11 era.

Anger is a self-protective emotion. We need the energy of anger to defend ourselves, but this same energy can be dangerous if it hardens into edginess. Judgment clouded by rage leads to exaggerated responses.[5]

---

4. Schachter and Singer, "Cognitive, Social and Physiological Determinants of Emotional State." Asch, "Opinions and Social Pressure."

5. Janis, *Groupthink.*

Furthermore we do not know how long our collective anger will last. Years? Decades? Will we give birth to new generations in the United States who will be raised on our story of 9/11 and locked into its anger so that they cannot live in peace with the children of those whom we judge were responsible for this tragedy? Do tragedies of this scope ever heal?

FEEDING ANGER TO KEEP IT ALIVE

In the United States we have a high level of anger fluency. Along with a powerful vocabulary for anger we have gestures, stances, and tones of voice to communicate that we are perturbed. In addition to expressing our own anger easily, we are primed to pick up the hostile cues of others. Signs of anger catch our attention; we are alert to them. Sarcasm, negativity, and disrespect are woven through conversations even at times when no one is particularly angry. It is part of a social style that communicates power. It is cool to be cynical. Perhaps it feels safe to hide inside the armor of an attitude that communicates "don't mess with me."

In mass entertainment anger is often linked with humor. There are social and legal limits to how far our anger may be acted out behaviorally, but almost no limits to how it may be expressed in the guise of humor or entertainment. We stop short of physical violence by making attacks with passive aggression, and we hide anger behind laughter when we engage in abrasive humor. No matter how we disguise it, however, it is still hostility.

In the generation of the Baby Boomers, *MAD* magazine, and the goofy face of Alfred E. Neuman taught us that we could laugh at everything. Nothing was sacred. The acronym *MAD*, which stands for "mutually assured destruction," reminds us that the things we laugh at are not always trivial. In the face of the ghastly prospect of nuclear war we covered up our vulnerability by laughing at the threat of extinction.

Dr. Strangelove was a box office hit in 1964. Its plot was built around the possibility that the United States and the Soviet Union would destroy each other when a berserk general determined to unleash his arsenal and set off the doomsday response of massive nuclear war. Many of us remember the image of bomber pilot, Major Kong, riding his warhead toward its target as he set off the chain reaction that would destroy the world. The idea was terrifying, but the movie images, though bizarre, were comical.

The Cold War divided the globe into two cohorts: the nations supporting the United States and those supporting the Soviet Union. During this ongoing rivalry we lived under a cloud of fear that the leaders of either side might be willing to put everything on the line and set off the battle that would result in our mutually assured destruction. We did not know the limits to which they would go in a showdown. It was not reassuring during the Cold War to hear loyal patriots say, "I would rather be dead than red." This was especially threatening because we were often reminded that each side had an arsenal of weapons powerful enough to destroy the world.

In the early 1960s homeowners built private fallout shelters just in case there was a nuclear event. The government also supported the development of community shelters in public buildings. In 1961 the Kennedy administration budgeted $100 million for building up civil defense.[6] When I was a student I lived in a residence hall with a deep basement. In one end of it there was a room that contained barrels stocked with emergency supplies to be used in case of a nuclear attack. We pushed these grim reminders of civic fear into the corner of the room and used the space for table tennis. At one and the same time we believed there was a threat, and we playfully ignored it.

Feelings of chronic fear can hide behind the bluff of anger. We would rather be angry than fearful in most cases because helpless fear feels empty while anger feels more alive. By stimulating our anger over and over again we stay keyed up, and these repetitions create an illusion of solidarity with others who are angry. Mental health professionals who treat clients for addiction also treat people who have become addicted to their anger. They get high on the adrenalin rush of anger; they feel alive, full of energy, and strong when they are angry. If they are not angry now and then they miss it. Like individuals our culture has many features of anger addiction.[7]

- We watch reality television shows in which people lie, cheat, and steal in order to advance themselves. We join vicariously in the showdown and choose sides. The passive act of watching turns into an emotional experience in which we too are competitors. We delight in the battle.

- We watch breaking news stories about natural disasters, pandemic health crises, shocking acts of gun violence, business leaders who turn out to be crooks, and ordinary citizens who turn out to be child predators. We have a steady diet of negatives. From what we see we assemble a negative impression of our own communities. To defend

6. Rose, *One Nation Underground*. Zacharias, "When Bomb Shelters Were All the Rage."

7. Real, *I Don't Want to Talk About It*, 147.

against our fear we armor ourselves with anger and build up suspicion of our neighbors.

- The average child in the United States witnesses 200,000 acts of violence on TV before reaching age eighteen. Preschool children confuse reality and fiction. If they conclude that their world is as dangerous as television, they may be frightened. If they conclude that violence is temporary and inconsequential, they may imitate it. There have been instances of young children bringing guns to school to settle grievances.

- We play videogames in which obliterating the enemy is the way to win. Eighty percent of children in the United States play videogames regularly. Studies of these children indicate that those exposed to video violence are more aggressive, less helpful, and more likely to see the world as hostile.

- Over half of all households in the United States have a gun; many people think of guns as security objects. We are used to watching dramas in which everything turns out okay when a gun-toting hero shows up. Actually, statistics show that the presence of a gun increases the risk of death by gunshot for the members of the household in which the gun is kept. Other studies indicate that after killing someone in the line of duty law enforcement and military personnel experience deep emotional distress. This is quite different from the gun fantasies we feed on while watching movies and television shows in which the killing of the villain is a great relief and is followed by a happily ever after closing scene.

- Anger is associated with power. Angry and aggressive persons get their way. In our culture we do not defend others against angry people. We are not likely to intervene, particularly if we think the aggression might get turned toward us.[8]

Individual anger and cultural anger may blend together so that an angry environment camouflages an angry individual. Familiarity with anger

---

8. Edelstein, "Tony Soprano, the Hero As Villain." Albert et al., "The Effect of Television News Valence on Arousal and Memory." Kerbel and Kerbel, *If it Bleeds, It Leads: An Anatomy of Television News.* Willenz, "Violent Videogames Can Increase Aggression." National Education Association Health Information Network, "Statistics: Gun Violence in Our Communities." Dutton, *The Abusive Personality: Violence and Control in Intimate Relationships.*

is both an individual pattern and a group habit. While we may recognize that our environment is hostile, we may not see how we contribute to that ourselves. It is difficult to sort out if we are angry so often because our environment is a frustrating place, or if our anger is a reflection of our own personal inclination to be provoked easily.

THE COST OF ANGER

Much of our personal anger is egocentric. It is triggered by threats to our self-esteem, our dignity, our convenience, or our opinion. We get angry about words, gestures, attitudes, and the behavior of others that discredit us. We judge motives. We assume that the person who offends us should have acted otherwise. Anger makes a claim on our attention. What if anger always has the last word so that it gradually becomes a familiar state? What if that anger stays with us and becomes part of our habitual disposition?

To measure our individual set points for anger we might compare our own attitudes to the attitudes of those around us. Or we might consider if our own set points for anger match the average set points in our culture. If we are living in a culture in which hostility is all around us, it is possible that we do not see it anymore. We are used to it; however, that does not decrease the price we pay for living in a state of chronic anger.

Anger is stressful. People who are stressed have higher levels of the chemicals the body manufactures to stay alert for trouble. Chronic stress may lead to coronary disease, hypertension, or other forms of illness. In an effort to control the agitation of chronic anger many persons abuse alcohol and drugs, indulge in emotional eating which is not healthy, or distract themselves with compulsive gambling or addictive sex. While addictions may temporarily relieve stress, in the long run they increase stress and exact a high price.

Anger keeps attention focused on power. The person who goes into life with a hostile view of the world collects offenses and expends effort defending against them. Beneath the anger is the fear that if you don't keep fighting, the dog eat dog world will chew you up and spit you out. Tragically, habits of hostility mobilize the negative feelings of others so that the hostile perception becomes a self-fulfilling prophecy. Habitually angry persons often fail to see what others need, what they intend, or even that they may be suffering. Rather than cooperating with others, anger-driven persons try to control others. Focused on control they are unable to see how their own behavior fuels the ongoing cycle of anger that eventually comes back at them. Chronic anger breeds isolation.[9]

We might say that life would be better if we lived in a culture less prone to anger. And we might say that we would have been better prepared for life if we had not experienced the frustrations of childhood and youth that left us with resentments. Of course there are those who have been wounded so deeply they cannot peel away their anger and go on with life as if the injury has not occurred. All of these things are true, but they are not ours to control. What is within our control is how we live with our own anger. We are responsible ourselves for the ways in which our unleashing of anger causes suffering. And no one is more accountable than we ourselves for the misery that living with stoked anger brings into our own lives and the happiness that it causes us to forfeit.

PRACTICING EQUANIMITY

We can decide to alter our dispositions. This does not mean that we ignore injustice, injury, or danger. Those things are real. But equanimity requires that we train ourselves not to add our own energy to the negative cycles of conflict. The first step in doing this involves taking ownership of our personal anger and not absorbing the mindless anger that is in the atmosphere of our culture. We can choose not to entertain ourselves with violence, play with anger, or blame others when we fail to control our own feelings. In the present discussion, we have moved back and forth several times between our cultural story and our individual narratives. Once again in the matter of anger we see that our culture gives us conflicting views.

On the one hand we are offered a view of anger without accountability. We are taught that anger is natural, that we are wired like the security system installed on a house. If no one is intruding, it will not go off. If it goes off, it is a sign that something wrong is being done to us. The other view of anger includes more accountability, but it is a view with which we often refuse to identify ourselves. When an enraged parent strikes a child, a partner batters a spouse, or a driver pulls a gun and shoots someone in a state

9. National Center for PTSD, "Anger and Trauma." Evces et al., "Effect of Trait Anger on Cognitive Processing of Emotional Stimuli." Potter-Efron, *Anger, Alcoholism, and Addiction.* Williams, *The Trusting Heart.* Hardy and Smith, "Cynical Hostility and Vulnerability to Disease: Social Support, Life Stress, and Physiological Response to Conflict." Donaldson and Flood, *Stop Hurting the Woman You Love.*

of road rage, we see it as anger gone too far. We describe these individuals as having "anger issues." That is a polite way of saying their trait anger is out of bounds, and they should do something about it. We like to think we are not like them.

Are we hard-wired for anger? Is it a natural emotion controlled by outside events? Some of the most useful research dealing with this matter has been conducted by a team of western scientists working in collaboration with the Dalai Lama in Tibet. They studied whether the propensity for anger is alterable and whether individuals can change the set point at which anger is triggered. The evidence strongly suggests that it is possible to alter the disposition for anger, and that we can retrain the brain structures and bodily reactions through which our anger is processed.[10] In the language of western science: we can alter our set point for anger. In the Dalai Lama's terms: we can discipline ourselves to be more compassionate.[11]

Staying balanced under stress requires preparing ourselves by calming our spirits and training our focus under ordinary circumstances. We learn peacefulness not when we are in the middle of conflict but when we are not. Practiced calm becomes a trait of character when we rehearse it daily. The permanence of our own anger, bitterness, and feelings of revenge are choices we make. Living in a state of peacefulness is similarly a choice.

Managing anger is not a choice to change someone else or fix the world; those options are not within the range of what is ours to control. But we can choose to steer our own course by tending to our own feelings. We can change our own readiness to act out anger, and we can develop daily habits of a peaceful disposition.

In his book, *Ethics for a New Millennium*, the Dalai Lama sets forth a compelling explanation for why we cannot be happy if we do not have compassion for others. Anger, he suggests, is an "afflictive emotion" that adds to suffering by either prompting us to add wrong to wrong or clouding our vision so that we cannot see that the compassionate way does not add to the injury or suffering of others.[12]

Compassion is not a light-hearted form of being nice, nor is it an unconsidered form of pity felt toward someone who is not as lucky as we are. It is a discipline, a way of thinking that is practiced, a way of acting that is intentional, and a way of managing our feelings that is rooted in the

10. Begley, *Train Your Mind, Change Your Brain*.
11. Goleman, *Destructive Emotions: How Can We Overcome Them?*
12. Dalai Lama, *An Open Heart: Practicing Compassion in Everyday Life*.

intent to live an ethical life so that we treat others with conscious regard for their humanity. Compassion is also essential to our own well-being. We do not have to abandon ourselves in order to be compassionate toward others. When we show concern for the well-being of others by being patient, forgiving, and kind, we also experience greater happiness ourselves.[13]

13. Dalai Lama, *Ethics for a New Millennium*, 127.

11

Recovering Attachments

Loyalty might be valuable, but is it viable?

—Eric Felten[1]

IN GENERATIONS PAST CHILDREN were groomed for relationships of adulthood. Family constituted an intimate circle of permanent contacts, and it was assumed that when children grew up they would create a second family with roles similar to those in their family of origin. The individuals who filled these roles shifted from one generation to the next, but the structure of the family remained the same.

Little boys were prepared to be providers. The word *husband* comes from the same root as the word *house*; a man's house was his castle.[2] In cooperation with a woman who was his helper a man created a home and had children. When he became a worker, a husband, and a father he achieved status as a man among other men. Many Baby Boomers who watched *Little House on the Prairie* thought Charles Ingalls was a nearly perfect man.

There was a matching apprenticeship for little girls. The role for which a girl was prepared revolved around being a wife to her husband, a mother to her children, and a homemaker. She needed a man to provide for her material needs, and she needed a mate with whom she could have children. In exchange she made his life comfortable, brought him status through the

1. Felten, *Loyalty: The Vexing Virtue*, 35.
2. *The Oxford English Dictionary*.

well-run household she created, and garnered honor for the family through the children she raised.

The family's division of labor, mandated by social convention, was seldom left to personal choice. It was customary for women who did not marry to remain in the family home and care for aging parents. These women, referred to disparagingly as old maids and spinsters, lived under a cloud of embarrassment for never having come to full adulthood. They were expected to be celibate, and often were treated as neurotic and flawed if they were.

Children were taught that being an old maid is not a good thing. The term itself was an insult. The card game *Old Maid* had one unmatched card, and the player who was stuck with this unpaired card at the end was the loser. Unpopped kernels at the bottom of the popcorn pan were also called old maids, and the implication was clear that they had not done what they were supposed to do. They were useless. Confirmed bachelors were less disparaged because employment outside the home gave them a social role. Nevertheless, creating the next generation of family was a pressing social duty for both men and women, and those who did not fulfill it were considered odd or incomplete.

In the 1960s Baby Boomers began to change their minds about family roles. Feminists protested that binding themselves to the work of the household and subordinating their lives to the agendas of their husbands made women second-class. Exclusion from the workplace, education, and the institutions of society caused women to be invisible, dependent, and powerless. Some men joined the protests, but mostly it was women who came together to work for Women's Liberation.

Women determined they would no longer accept gender limitations. They stopped calling each other *girls* and insisted on being called *women*. As consciousness shifted, grammar changed. Referring to human beings by the generic term *man* or referring to an unnamed individual as *he* was no longer acceptable. Many women chose not to give up their own surnames to take their husbands' when they married. Institutional cultures, the law, and public attitudes that defined gender in the United States went through a drastic revision.

Women who witnessed doors opening to them where once they had been closed learned an indelible lesson about the costs of prejudice and the power of opportunity. They refused to repeat the patterns that had defined the lives of their mothers and grandmothers. For themselves and their daughters they envisioned a different future. Remodeling the roles of men and women in society also meant changing the meaning of intimacy.

WHEN INTIMACY WAS PRIVACY

Traditional households into which many Baby Boomers were born placed high value on a circle of private relationships that lasted for a lifetime. The family was both the unit of intimacy and a sanctuary of privacy, and boundaries between private life and public life were important. Outside the family circle people were known to each other by their roles: employees of companies, participants in organizations, or residents in a neighborhood. Family members shared the status of the head of the household, the man. Assembled around his identity was a cluster of other family identifiers: ethnic or class membership, a network of social associations (religious affiliation, school, clubs), and the family's economic status.

In contrast to the family's public identity, life within the domestic circle was protected from outside scrutiny. It was private, and that shelter constituted a style of intimacy based on loyalty. Outside the safety of the family discretion was necessary because members of the traditional family were obliged to protect the reputation of the family. They were cautious about discussing things that happened at home. These expectations extended also to children who were taught early on that they should be seen and not heard in adult company. For better or worse, their behavior was a reflection of their family. Furthermore there was a risk that a child who talked too freely would be indiscreet and reveal matters that were supposed to stay sheltered inside the family.

During the 1950s many American households watched *Art Linkletter's House Party* on television. On his show Linkletter drew children into conversation so that they would say aloud things that were meant to be kept private. Naïve comments about their parents or family secrets entertained viewers. Although Linkletter was breaking the old-fashioned rule that children should be seen but not heard, he did so tactfully. The children's disclosures appeared unintended, and Linkletter softened them with the grandfatherly observation that "kids say the darndest things."

Comparing Linkletter's program to shows that came later illustrates the changes that took place in domestic privacy within just a few decades. The *House Party* was phased out in 1967 and replaced by shows like Bob Eubank's *Newlywed Game*. The indiscretions of Linkletter's children were mild in comparison to the exhibitionism of adults interviewed by Eubanks whose questions about "whoopee" encouraged couples to reveal details about sex.

Standards for what was attention-getting, humorous, and publicly acceptable have been changing ever since. In the first decade of the new millennium television viewers are allowed to be spectators at private events like surgeries, arrests, family quarrels, and intimate moments between bachelors and bachelorettes as they turn courting into a competitive sport broadcast on reality television. Personal discretion is a thing of the past, but also family privacy and keeping the confidences of friends and colleagues is no longer a strong social expectation.

The value of discretion has been replaced by admiration for transparency. In 1978, when Christina Crawford wrote *Mommie Dearest,* it was still shocking that a child would write a tell-all memoir about her mother and put it on display for anyone who wanted to know about the shadow side of a Hollywood star like Joan Crawford.[3] Three decades later tell-all memoirs are a genre in their own right. Barbara Walters, who was second to none in getting famous people to drop their guard and reveal what they had been holding back, finally revealed her own story in *Audition,* which was published in 2008.[4]

Traditional expectations for privacy covered more than scandal. In 1974 Betty Ford, the wife of then President Gerald Ford, revealed to the public that she had undergone surgery for breast cancer. Her disclosure was daring because she was an attractive woman and the treatment had required the removal of her breast. Betty Ford determined that she would break through the barriers of public modesty that inhibited other women from seeking the treatment they needed for a life-threatening disease. Pulling aside the curtain of privacy that shielded a significant event in the life of her own family allowed Betty Ford to advocate for cancer screening. Now just a few decades later it is difficult to imagine that anyone would be secretive about an illness like breast cancer.

Our understanding of privacy no longer has much to do with preserving our dignity. Where it functions at all, it is usually to protect our economic interests. The health care industry has been forced to keep our medical information private so that our prospects for employment and insurance are not jeopardized. We shred bank statements and conceal our

3. Crawford, *Mommie Dearest.*

4. Walters, *Audition.*

PINs so no one can tamper with our accounts, steal our money, or ruin our credit. At the same time callers to radio talk shows broadcast the most private information about themselves to thousands of other listeners. The public is interested in whether the President wears boxers or briefs. On Facebook personal news, pictures, and profiles get widely distributed to a circle of acquaintances, some of whom are barely known, but still are called "friends."

SIGNIFICANT OTHERS

In 2004 Tim Russert, then the moderator of *Meet the Press*,[5] wrote a memoir about his father whom he called "Big Russ." In explaining his reason for writing *Big Russ and Me* Russert tells of taking part in an online conversation in which someone asked him to name the individual who more than any other he would like to interview. Russert writes:

> The person who submitted that question was probably expecting me to name an elusive political figure, or perhaps a fascinating figure from history, such as Thomas Jefferson, Christopher Columbus, or my first choice, Jesus Christ. But I took the question personally, and answered it immediately and from my heart: more than anyone else, I would like to interview my dad.[6]

Tim's relationship with Big Russ was built on trust and respect. He admired the principles by which his father lived, and he believed he had character. Tim absorbed the steady image of his father and carried it with him like a talisman. In the language of psychology this is called *introjection*, and the person with this profound influence is called a *significant other*. These role models leave a deep impression on children because they teach them life lessons and help them define themselves. A person who serves this role is a permanent fixture in a child's consciousness.

In the course of the Boomer generation we stopped honoring the significant others who had helped us grow up. If we concerned ourselves with introjections at all it was usually so we could excise the damage our parents had caused by not being perfect. We resented the bad memories we carried with us due to their mistakes. We dug into our psyches to expose how our

5. Tim Russert passed away suddenly from a heart attack on June 13, 2008. His aging father outlived him.

6. Russert, "Excerpt from *Big Russ and Me*."

parents had made us codependent, how they had damaged our self-esteem, and what unresolved family issues were still blocking our path to freedom and happiness. When our own relationships did not work, we pointed an accusing finger at our parents.

While we were taking the significant others of our pasts down from their pedestals, we were also recycling the term we used to refer to them. *Significant other* now came to refer to a different kind of relationship we have with those who are at the top of our priority list. Most of these are lovers, life partners, or spouses. To be significant the relationship does not need to have a history, and in some cases it also does not need to have a future. It has to be current and important.

Because the new style of significant relationship usually begins with enchantment (falling in love, infatuation, sexual attraction), many of them do not become permanent unless they can move beyond that stage into something more stable. We break up with significant others if the relationship does not work out during dating. We divorce them if we happened to marry, and later it turns sour. No matter how important they have been in the past, it is considered unhealthy to let them continue as significant others after a breakup. When we find new relationships to replace our failed ones, we are expected to get over our exes.

Changing expectations for the people who hold the most important positions in our lives are reflected in the language we now use to describe them. Persons who form a romantic pair may be referred to as spouse, mate, life partner, domestic partner, or significant other. Increasingly, however, these persons are referred to simply as *partners*. They are our significant others. Prior to the Baby Boomer generation a partner was a business associate, someone to team up with in sports, the person on the same team in a card game, or the other dancer when people still danced in pairs. Today the term refers to a sexual pairing. If someone asks you how many partners you have had in your adulthood they probably are not asking about business or playing bridge.

The terms *husband* and *wife* also are becoming passé because practical considerations like money, lifestyle, or social commitments are simplified if partners do not marry or live together. If they do not intend to have children they may not think it necessary to make the partnership legal. These are personal choices, and increasingly they are accepted as a matter of course. The generic term *partner* may refer to tonight's date or a long-term relationship. Furthermore a man's partner could be another man, and a woman's partner could be another woman. Even if a couple chooses to marry, referring to them as partners is a way of sidestepping any suggestion of status differences between men and women. A term that fits all cases avoids the embarrassing blunders that occur if we try to be too specific.

A lot rests on freestanding partnerships if they are disconnected from supportive social structures and extended family. The way adults relate to their parents, siblings, and relatives has become tentative. We can choose to let them be important, but just as easily we can sideline them. The same goes for the families of our partners. We only have to deal with them if we like them, and it all depends on what we want for ourselves.

The remaining candidate for the role of significant other is the partner, but when other relationships are minimized that creates high-pressure expectations. Can one person be a financial advisor, a social buddy, a coparent, a roommate sharing a living space, a sexual partner, a loyal caretaker in times of distress, and a source of deep emotional connection? Not only does it seem like too much to expect from one person, it also seems like too much to provide to someone else. For that reason partners often claim the freedom to determine what they will and what they will not include in their relationship agreement. Many partnerships are tailor-made.

Despite all these complications, having a partner still is perceived by most people as a good thing. What kind of partner to choose or what kind of agreement to make is an open choice, but having one still means you are not alone in the world. With the fading importance of other forms of attachment, that single most significant attachment, even if it is temporary, is an important anchor point for many people.

The option of relinquishing significant others who are disappointing, whether they are family, friends, or love interests, has an element of frankness to it. In a free culture we don't have to pretend that people are important to us if in fact they aren't, but these changes have hidden costs. When we are alienated from persons who were once significant to us, we lose a part of ourselves. We let go of someone who remembers what we were like when we were young, remembers the birth of children, the death of parents, significant things that happened in the lives of friends, important accomplishments, places we have lived before, or adventures we shared. Splitting off from people who have been important in our past involves retelling our history to make sense of the changes. It takes maturity to make this a step in the direction of telling the truth about ourselves; more often it is an occasion for telling the cold hard truth about those who are now less important to us than they used to be.

The changes that the Boomer generation brought about in their vision of relationships have left us with hard questions. Who are our significant others? How important are honest relationships for our own process of maturity? Who are the people in our lives who really know us? Where can we find intimacy? Where can we find constancy? What is the value of loyalty, and what happens to us if we try to live without it?

FAUX INTIMACY

As we became more tentative about traditional roles we also began to describe relationships in more individualistic terms. A strong individual with good social skills can pick and choose. We now speak admiringly of someone who is transparent or unguarded, but we are just as likely to admire someone who has good boundaries. In the 70s and 80s we became more public about ourselves, and since the 90s we have become hyper-connected to each other by technology. In a world in which we are constantly dealing with others and a little uncertain about the risks we are taking, choosing our relationships and controlling how involved we allow them to be is a way of preserving ourselves.

Although we are connected all the time, many of our communications lack depth and intimacy. Not long ago I noticed three young women at one of the other tables in the coffee shop. As they chatted with each other one or another of them would break out of the conversation and read, text, or scroll through messages on her phone. Finally at one point they were all busy on their phones. Like many of us, they had trouble being where they were because they were everywhere at once. In the heavy traffic of communication we have little time to pause and think, and even less time to pause and share anything more than our fleeting thoughts with others. We are always on the move.

As our lives have less and less real intimacy of the kind that invites us to pause, to think about the meaning of what we are doing, and to share our reflections with each other, we find substitutes for intimacy. These stand-ins are to intimacy what sugar substitutes are to nutrition. They have a vague resemblance, but they are not the real thing. Temporarily they may fill our longing for connection, but because they do not offer real intimacy, we do not flourish when we indulge in them.

We consume stories about intimacy in film, on the news, and in books we read. Some of these vicarious experiences are more interesting than our own lives. They wake us up. Life shattering disasters or great love affairs spice our imaginations. We can watch breaking news as it is happening. Technology gives us images so vivid we feel we can reach out and touch them. Briefly it feels like our own story. But it isn't. No matter how vivid and intriguing the story, we are still only spectators.

We may feel connected to someone else when we are deeply moved. Intensity is easily mistaken for intimacy. All over the world audiences watched spellbound as thirty-three Chilean miners made the fifteen minute journey one at a time from their prison deep under the earth to the surface and their waiting families. We were choked up. We felt as if we had gotten to know them personally as we waited for their rescue, always entertaining the possibility that something could go wrong and "we" would lose them.

Some of the miners made promises about how their lives would be different after this experience, and we understood what prompted them to do that. They had gone through a life-changing event. Watching them as spectators was enough to inspire us to make resolutions of our own. I personally know one mother who on that very day called her children to tell them how much she loved them lest she miss the opportunity and something should happen to one of them.

There is no debating that what happened to the miners and what happened to us as we watched them was deeply moving. But it was not intimate because even if we felt we got to know them personally, they did not know us. With telephoto lenses we probed into the touching moments when they were reunited with their loved ones. They did not look back at us. We were anonymous viewers, nameless among the millions of others like us who were tuned in to watch the drama unfold. Their intimacy was not ours.

We may mistake popularity for intimacy. Being known a little by many people does not add up to being known well by anyone. Being well-known and known well are not the same. Performers can draw energy from a cheering audience, and they feel the difference between a full house and an empty auditorium. Sometimes they claim they feel an intimate connection with the audience, but this is not real intimacy. Performers do not know one admirer from another when they look out into the sea of anonymous faces.

Approval has magnetism. We notice people who like us, and we may feel drawn to them. It does not follow, though, that those who know us best are those who approve of us most. Or we might turn it around and say that those who approve of us most are not necessarily those who know us best. In the real rough and tumble of relationships it is usually the case that those who know us best also have seen us at our worst. They know our weaknesses, mistakes, and bad habits. And they stay with us because they are bonded with us in a truly intimate way. It is a gift not dependent on perfection or idealization.

Gaining access by stealth to what is private also may feel like intimacy. Reading someone's diary, using pornography, or listening in on a private conversation may be intriguing. If loneliness or isolation fuels the drive to find a way into the privileged part of someone else's life, these brief intrusions may even give momentary relief. But voyeurism is not intimacy, because what has been taken has not been given knowingly to the one who takes it. It is a deceit.

Exhibitionism also is not intimacy because it is a manipulation of the witness. It brings to mind a young woman who posted indiscreet images of herself on the Internet. When asked if she was concerned what others would think of her when they saw them she replied: "They can just accept me the way I am, and if they can't, well screw them." The exhibitionist does not care who sees, but in real intimacy we care deeply. Because the exhibitionist has no private self, the disclosures soon become boring unless new or forbidden ways to be even more daring are found.

Millions of viewers in the United States watched six seasons of *Sex and the City*, the story of four women living in New York. They are attractive women and have no difficulty finding partners for sex. Their alliances come and go while the most reliable source of intimacy for all four women is their friendship with the other three. Many men discounted the show because watching a "chick flick" made them uncomfortable, but many women watched this show with envy because for a few minutes during each installment they were allowed to imagine what it would be like to have three friends who stand by loyally while you navigate the currents of your life.

What makes a relationship good? Which relationships hold up through change? Can they weather misunderstandings? Does attachment grow as a result of being together over time? Is sex without intimacy durable? Do children seal the deal? What does real intimacy offer that we cannot find in the psychodramas of faux intimacy?

WHAT IS INTIMACY?

There is no short road to intimacy. Safe relationships are built on the foundation of moral conviction. The conditions we put forth in genuine encounters of intimacy are not what we demand of others; they are the standards to which we hold ourselves. We put them forth when we invite others to count on us, and included in those standards is the promise that when we fall short of the covenant we have made, we will open ourselves to be reminded of that to which we have already committed ourselves. Moral principles that guide us in our relationships do not dictate the specifics of our actions, nor do they condemn us to a narrow and uncreative life. They stand as measures by which we assess the spirit of our own actions in relation to those to whom we have promised loyalty.

Intimacy is a spiritual space in which we give our full attention to others without violating them by our own impulse to control, correct, or reshape them according to our own liking. Being an intimate witness of others requires that we create a space of respect. We hold others in regard by honoring their dignity even at times when they are struggling to maintain it. We hold hope for them when they are shaken. When they are weak or threatened we stand by them. We do this without covering up what is disappointing or unattractive. We do not look away. In an intimate relationship we see each other openly, for better or for worse, knowing we will see both, and at the same time we remain committed to nurturing the best in each other.

Intimacy is more than insurance for tough times. In the sanctuary of intimacy we also celebrate life's milestones together. We affirm each other's efforts to accomplish what is worthwhile. We savor life's delights together. And in the best of times we magnify each other's joy by being there to echo it. When we offer this sacred space to others our own lives are extended because together we can experience far more than we can experience alone. When another sees us honestly in this safe space, our understanding of the meaning of our own life is deepened. We are freed from the narrowness of a life focused primarily on self.

We cannot honor intimacy unless we also honor solitude. Intimacy is not something that we can have on demand. Sometimes we will be alone. Learning to calm ourselves in solitude, to tune out the distractions that are constantly bidding for our attention, teaches us how to create sanctuary for ourselves when we are alone. It also teaches us how to create sanctuary for those with whom we are intimate when we are together. We need sanctuary to unpack our own spiritual questions, and to bring to light our concerns about the meaning of life. In solitude we create sanctuary for ourselves; in intimacy we share that sanctuary with others.

Just as it is the case that we cannot see our own faces unless we have something to show us our reflection, so there are also things about ourselves we will not understand until we see ourselves in the safe and intimate presence of others. Those with whom we share the safe haven of intimacy nurture us in our search for meaning. They are our significant others.

12

Seasoned by Care

Work is love made visible.

—KHALIL GIBRAN[1]

M Y YOUNG FRIEND NICK recently spent two hours on a Saturday afternoon moving a woodpile from the edge of the woods to the door of the cabin. He knew he was accomplishing something worthwhile because wood is needed for heating the cabin when the sun goes down and it gets cool inside. Nick did not ask if the woodpile was his chore to do. I doubt that any of the adults present would have asked a seven-year-old to spend two hours moving a woodpile.

Nick willingly did a task that benefited others. He worked without complaint as if he enjoyed the task, and his generous effort suggests he knew his helpfulness defined a role for him in the group. Developmental theorists tell us there is an age between six and twelve when children discover work. Preschool children enjoy being helpers because they like sharing a task with an adult, but at the optimal age for learning about work children become interested in the task for its own sake. Once children discover industry, they can accomplish a great deal if they are motivated.[2]

Some rewards for work come from the outside. They are *extrinsic rewards*. My dog understands extrinsic rewards. He will lie down, roll over,

1. Gibran, *On Work*.
2. Erikson, *Identity and the Life Cycle*.

shake, stay, and heel if I have dog treats in my pocket. As far as I know my dog never practices on his own when I am not around. There is nothing to indicate that he makes plans or sets goals for himself. I doubt that his conscience would be uneasy if he helped himself to a treat from a box left within his reach because he is not able to judge whether or not he deserves it. Neither sloth nor industry are much concern to him; after all, he's a dog.

A second type of motivation comes from *intrinsic rewards*. These are rewards from engaging in behavior that has a purpose that we believe has merit. Mihalyi Csikszentmihalyi is an American psychologist who has studied what happens to people when they are in a state of *flow*, a state of being so absorbed with an activity that the discomfort of putting forth effort drops away and there is a simple harmony between the task and the one who performs it. Csikszentmihalyi observed that people are happy in this state of flow; time flies and other concerns seem to recede. Work done in this state is fulfilling for its own sake.[3]

Csikszentmihalyi uses the concept of an autotelic self to refer to an individual who is able to turn most challenges and even adversities into something positive. He suggests that in order to do this it is necessary to recognize the challenge and set a goal, then to become deeply involved in the pursuit of the goal while keeping attention focused on it, and to do this in a way that is not purely egocentric but rather woven together into those values and goals that orient one's life.

In research on flow experience researchers found that there were far more such experiences at work than during leisure for most of the individuals they studied, and they also found that subjects reported they are happier when in a state of flow, i.e., when in a state of being immersed in an activity. At the same time most workers said they preferred time off from work to time at work. In making some initial conjectures about the cause of this paradox Csikszentmihalyi suggests that the difference in attitude about work and leisure may be related to the fact that work often does not seem voluntary while leisure is. The matter of a self-selected goal may make a difference.

Sometimes what we accomplish through work is only a temporary benefit. It is not long after the meal just prepared that the family is hungry again, and the laundry just done is back in the hamper. Many tasks are ongoing and never done completely, but despite this there can be satisfaction

3. Csikszentmihalyi, *Flow*.

in doing them. It is possible to learn respect for work so that no matter how humble the task, it feels better to do it well than to do it poorly.

In the Boomer generation there was a sharp shift in perception of work. Ideas vigorously discussed among leaders of the New Left first focused on politics and economics, but gradually they spilled over into other areas of life: family, education, gender relations, and non-governmental institutions.[4] New views of labor, wealth, rights, and the distribution of American prosperity were raised as a challenge to practices current at the time. The relationship of employee to employer was cast in an adversarial frame. Families caught in ongoing cycles of poverty became a cause for critics who believed the economic system was intrinsically unjust.

Ideas that originated with intellectuals were taken up by activists in the streets and by young people who were reacting against the lifestyles of their parents. They protested that work locked people into conformity because income was necessary to sustain a middle-class way of life. Stepping off the economic treadmill meant dropping out of the contest of those striving to "keep up with the Joneses." Because work required submission to authority structures, social critics protested that it was contrary to freedom.

To take a stand against the economic Establishment many activists advocated "principled poverty," which meant not working for an employer, not acquiring possessions, and not observing the restraints on behavior that defined what was socially acceptable in a conformist society. In some cases this was as simple as men not shaving, cutting their hair, showering, or wearing shoes, or women not wearing makeup, using deodorant, styling their hair or wearing bras. In other cases it meant dropping out, getting high, and living a bohemian lifestyle. This appealed to young and disenchanted Americans who had not yet taken up adult obligations because an alternative lifestyle did not require sacrifice on their part so much as resistance to taking the steps that were expected of them as they entered adulthood.

Like much of the youth culture of the 1960s, the protest movements of the time slowly dissolved and their adherents assimilated back into the mainstream. However, some of the values formed in the 1960s still hold sway in attitudes toward work. What if I put in more than I get back, does that mean I am being exploited? Why should I do more than anyone else

4. Jamison and Eyerman, *Seeds of the Sixties*. The authors identify intellectuals who were able to influence the political and ideological views of young and disenchanted Americans: C. Wright Mills, Hannah Arendt, Erich Fromm, Herbert Marcuse, Margaret Mead, and others.

does? What right does someone else have to expect me to do work I don't like?

In the folk ethic of the past the purpose of work was for each adult to do a fair share of the labor required to advance family, community, and nation. Whether or not people actually lived up to this ideal is another matter; what is identified here is the standard most people accepted as the common view. Respect for "the work ethic" was the expectation they felt in the culture around them. As the ideals of freedom and individual rights gained ascendancy during the 1970s, the meaning of work became more individual. It was widely accepted that all persons should have the opportunity to work as much as they need to in order to get the things they want. This did not imply an obligation on the part of individuals to advance the common good, nor did it imply personal responsibility. Rather it suggested that individuals should have what they want.

The value of work is no longer clear in our culture. Do we avoid it whenever possible? Do we tolerate it only when it is necessary? Is having a "work ethic" old-fashioned? Is having a job a right? Do we respect people who do their work well?[5]

SLOBS AND SLOTH

My friend Dave told me of an incident that occurred when he went with his father and his son for a football weekend. The three of them stayed in a hotel room together. When the sixteen-year-old was ready to brush his teeth he spit his gum into the sink. His grandfather asked him to clean up the gum, but the boy replied that housekeeping would do it. "That's what they get paid for," he said.

This was the wrong thing for a sixteen-year-old kid to say to his eighty-year-old grandfather who in his youth had done every humble job offered him. He peeled potatoes in a restaurant. He worked extra weekend shifts in a factory. There were bills to pay, and meeting those obligations was essential to his self-respect. Time has passed and he is financially secure now, but he still has no tolerance for laziness. Dave knew that the boy's comment offended his grandfather, and the older man was known to say cruel things. As he left the room his parting comment was, "You're a slob."

5. Gladwell, *Outliers: The Story of Success.* Colvin, *Talent is Overrated: What Really Separates World-Class Performers From Everybody Else?* Ericcson, "Expert Performance and Deliberate Practice."

He was disappointed that his own grandson would think work was beneath him, especially work that he had created by his own carelessness.

There is a stark contrast between Dave's son and Dave's dad. Dave's dad sees work as a badge of honor. His grandson sees it as a burden, something he wants to avoid if he can. Dave's dad had life experiences that proved the value of work. Dave's son expects to get everything he wants without work. His parents will float loans to send him to college. They will assure him a place to live, a car, a computer, a phone, and much else. In the value system by which Dave's dad lives, sloth is a flaw of character, because when one person is lazy others have to do a greater share. Even in an age of plenty he does not buy into the notion that it is acceptable for some people to be providers so others can be consumers. In his grandson's frame of reference dodging work is freedom.

INTENTIONAL CARING

Work is more than labor, it is more than employment, and it is more than duty. Central to the meaning of work is effort, and this is true regardless of where, for whom, or why work is done. It is a school for character. When we are working we are *putting forth effort for good purposes*, and in the process we are also receiving something of value because we are learning to *care*. The ability to care for something other than ourselves opens up the world for us and lets us discover, with some relief, that the universe does not revolve around us. Consider this statement: "I care for things I care for."

In the English language the word *care* has two meanings. The one meaning of care is to provide for someone or something. For example, we might say that the teacher took care of the students on their trip. The other meaning of the word expresses the value of a person or thing. I care very much for my young friend Nick. He does not require much caretaking anymore, but I care about him very much. The two meanings of the same word highlight the two sides of our responsible connection to people and things. These two meanings also reflect the essence of work. We take care, and we care about.

I have a garden where I pull weeds and water plants, put in new perennials, trim and prune when the season dictates, and put compost around plants to feed them. Why do I garden? I take care of the growing things in my garden *because I care about them*. It is just as true that I care about the things in my garden *because* I have taken care of them? I wonder if I would find as much delight in my garden if I had never worked in it or if I neglected it because I became too busy with other things.

The connection between taking care of something and caring about it is not dependent on ownership. Caring for something does not make it mine. I do not cherish the flowers in my garden because I own them. I cherish them because I *know* them. In caring for them I observe them closely, and I appreciate them because they are familiar to me. Working in my garden lets me see the marvel of living things. I watch a root that is frozen solid all winter warm up in the spring and produce a tender string of bleeding hearts. My garden, which is withered and brown all winter, turns into a showcase of colors, textures, and shapes when spring comes. I muse about how the flowers share the space with rabbits, butterflies, birds, as well as the sun and rain and wind. We all share it too with the deer that in the winter chewed the bark off a tree I planted last fall.

What I experience with my garden the farmer may experience with a herd, the politician with social policy, the human rights activist with justice, the environmentalist with the river, the medical worker with the patient, and adoring parents with a newborn baby. The world offers infinite ways in which we may care about it and care for it. The two sides of caring are almost always linked. The more I take care, the more I care. When we find a place where we can invest our efforts in caring for something, we also uncover a sense of purpose. And when our efforts serve a purpose beyond our own interests, our world is expanded.

CARING, A DECISION OR A HABIT

It is hard to appreciate something we neglect because it reflects our care-lessness back to us. Instead of using something we waste it. Instead of appreciating something we ignore it. Instead of preserving something we consume it. We become estranged from things we neglect. It is difficult to take something seriously if we do not bother to notice it, and it is difficult to cherish things for which we are not willing to make effort. The things for which we fail to exercise care fall out of the circle of our concern.

Freedom gives us the option of not caring about many things. That is what we imply when we say, "It's not my problem." It is what we do when we choose not to involve ourselves with things by which we do not want to be burdened. These choices have consequences. Detachment from activity that has purpose and meaning shrinks our world. We know it less well, and we have less of a place in it.

NEVER TOO OLD TO CARE

In 1921 the psychologist Lewis Terman recruited 1,500 boys and girls to take part in a study of gifted children. In addition to testing their IQ Terman gathered information about many areas of their lives. Until Terman's death in 1956, when his original participants were in their forties, he continued to gather detailed information about them. Fortunately others continued the work Terman began, and the few remaining survivors of the original participant group have now passed the century mark.

Howard Friedman and Leslie Martin head a team of researchers at the University of California, Riverside. They have mined the Terman data and added much of their own in order to investigate factors that appear to be related to longevity. In 2011 they published their results in *The Longevity Project*. One of the most striking results of their study was the discovery that the rankings parents and teachers gave for how conscientious a child was turned out to be the strongest predictor of longevity. The most conscientious lived the longest.

Children who had high conscientiousness ratings were those who controlled their impulsivity and were responsible. Many of these participants maintained their habits of conscientiousness into adulthood. They were productive and diligent, created healthy work situations for themselves, and formed good relationships at work. Being cooperative with others was part of mastering the challenges of work.

Even as they aged the conscientious subjects of Friedman and Martin's study continued to be productive individuals. Whether still employed, retired and working for social causes, or pursuing hobbies or education they continued to be disciplined in setting goals and pursuing them. In the study report they are described as prudent, dependable, and persevering.

Friedman and Martin must know that there are negative stereotypes about people who are too diligent and work too hard. But Friedman and Martin take a strong stand and insist, "people who have meaningful and important jobs and who are especially productive are much happier than those who are unpressured, lackadaisical slackers. . . . And they not only stay healthier but they are happier to boot."[6]

6. Friedman and Martin, *The Longevity Project (Kindle ed.)*, 2431–32.

As Boomers begin to reach retirement age they see ahead of them a stage of life during which they may not be employed. The structure of their days may be altered and the sources of their income may shift. Many of the responsibilities that once took their time and energy will be passed along to others. Many of the children Boomers raised are now parents raising their own children. The households Boomers ran may have become simpler and smaller. They may have less physical stamina than they once did. Does this mean they are phasing out the stage of life during which work, effort, and caring are important? Does it mean they are destined to be slackers?

If the meaning of work in our lives has been entirely focused on our own financial gain, our own status and success, our own accumulation of the means for getting what we want, then our days of work may well be over. If work has been a burdensome means to an end, then leaving it may be a relief, but the relief will create a void. What will we do with our time? How will we find purpose, interest, and meaning with which to fill our days?

If work has been integrated into our lives so that it has shaped our character and taught us the satisfaction of exerting effort to good ends, it will continue as a habit. We will care about new things, and we will find new ways to enact our caring. The means by which we care may become less exerting, quieter, and simpler. Still we will be able to care. The ways in which we have cared and that for which we have cared will have shaped our disposition. It will continue to direct our energies so that we can find purpose in putting effort to good ends. This is particularly so if we have practiced working with intention and diligence, if we have made it our habit to show concern for people and things in whatever way we are able. If we have come to understand the value of that, then work merges with care, and care can have the last word.

When I think of a person who understood the meaning of work, I think of my own mother. She was the last child in a large family and lost her mother at a young age. The family soldiered its way through the Great Depression by pooling resources, and the children took whatever work they could find. My mother was no stranger to work. One could honestly say her character had been formed by work. She cared about many things and was competent in many ways, and for those things about which she cared she gave of herself tirelessly.

When my mother was ninety-two she taught me one more lesson about doing what you do well. She had suffered a stroke and was in nursing care by then. One autumn weekend I decided to take her to the north country one more time. I packed her into the back seat of the car and propped her up with pillows so she would not fall over if she dozed, and I crawled in next to her. My husband and my father sat in the front chatting about cars and listening to the radio. By this time my mother's thinking was not very clear, but she seemed to enjoy riding and viewing the autumn colors. At one point she said, "The trees are so beautiful and there are so many." She was trying to make conversation with me. She wanted to be good company. I think she knew it was a slightly odd comment, because she gave me a pained and puzzled grin.

We stayed in a small motel, and I had to help her because she could not dress herself or take herself to the bathroom anymore. As we were doing the morning routines she seemed sad, and I asked her why. She said she wished she could do more. It bothered her that she could no longer take care of herself or anyone else. That is how she had spent her life, and it had meant a great deal to her.

I tried to reassure my mother that caring for her was not hard because she was always appreciative. She cooperated however she could, and she never complained. And then, perhaps on a whim, I said to her, "Mom, you can do something. You can be good to take care of." The look on her face remains with me to this day. My mother had coal black eyes and a halo of white hair. And out of her haze she gazed at me, her brow wrinkled up the way an infant's does who is trying to figure out something that she can't quite understand. Then I could see the light go on, and she smiled. "Well, I can certainly do that," she said. She seemed relieved, and her mood brightened. I believe she was comforted because her commitment to life, to always do the best she could, was back in place.

13

Reclaiming the Sacred Circle

Religious and moral truths, even if long discovered,
must always be re-discovered; and they are re-discovered,
not just by being re-thought but by being re-lived.

—EMIL FACKENHEIM[1]

DURING THE FINANCIAL CRISIS of the 2000s the news flooded us with stories about bankers and CEOs who lined their pockets while stockholders stood by helplessly watching the value of their own assets plummet. On a single day the *New York Times* posted several articles exposing executive greed. One reported generous compensation packages for executives of Freddie Mac and Fannie May. During a time that careless business practices were causing immense liability for taxpayers, the executives continued to benefit without penalty. A second article appeared on the same day reporting enormous compensation for hedge fund managers in a year when the actual returns for the funds were weak. The sum of the twenty-five highest compensation packages for managers was 22 billion dollars. Yes, that is with a "b."

It frightens the public to discover that people running companies whose stock we own or in whose care our retirement funds have been placed are unconcerned about us. They are not building their company's security, increasing benefits for employees, bringing prosperity to the

1. Fackenheim, *Quest for Past and Future: Essays in Jewish Theology*, 140.

community, or rewarding stockholders' investments. They are just getting rich themselves, and in the process they are making our futures insecure.[2]

Most of these leaders of the financial world are Boomers. They are part of a generation whose folk ethic promotes self-love as a good thing; their sense of freedom allows them to assert shamelessly that their first duty is to themselves. Many others as well affirm those attitudes when applied to themselves; however, when they are helpless consumers and self-centered values are used against them, it changes the picture. In defense of our own interests we quickly appeal to moral standards and revile the selfishness of those whose choices put us at a disadvantage. We want to believe that if we were in their shoes, we would behave differently. But would we? Might we also justify our own strivings by setting morality aside and accepting that the less stringent limits of the law are good enough?

Jean Twenge is a psychologist who describes the attitudes and life-styles of young people born since the 1970s. Because shifts in the identity of this group show an increase in narcissism, she calls them "the Me Generation" or "the Entitlement Generation." Many of the attitudes Twenge traces first surfaced among Baby Boomers and have been carried over to their children. Recurring attitude surveys indicate that with each succeeding decade those coming of age, after being nurtured by the limitless affirmations of Boomer parents, are more concerned with self and more lacking in empathy for others.

Members of the "Me Generation" are less likely than their parents or grandparents to join organizations and associations that require commitment. Their networks are opportunistic, they are easily altered by changing circumstances when people move away, change jobs, break up with partners, or move into new circles of friends. The lifestyles of self-focused individuals do not sustain relationships of family, marriage, friendship, and community unless it is to their own benefit.

Twenge finds a high level of distress in the age groups she studies. They feel their lives are controlled by circumstances, a factor she calls "externality." The profile of the Me Generation shows increases in depression, suicide, the use of antidepressants, and mental health treatment for anxiety and stress. They have an abundance of confidence about how special they are, but they have little on which to count that serves as an anchor for them.

2. Morgenson, "Report Criticizes High Pay at Fannie and Freddie." Creswell, "Even Funds That Lagged Paid Richly."

Many of the subjects interviewed for Twenge's studies say they are lonely. Something very basic is lacking in their lives.[3]

ALONE OR TOGETHER

Researchers who study cultural differences in social expectations identify two patterns for balancing concern for self with concern for others. These patterns go by various names. *Egocentric* or *sociocentric*. *Individualist* or *collectivist*. Some researchers use simpler terms, such as *I* or *We orientations*, to describe these social arrangements. And still others, looking for more neutral terms, call the two systems *independent* or *interdependent*. The American pattern leans strongly toward being egocentric, individualist, and I-oriented. We value independence over interdependence.[4]

As our contacts become more global, Americans are introduced to people from other cultures who question the individualism of our lifestyles. They prod us to consider if the good life is to be found by pursuing what we want for ourselves and measuring contentment by our personal satisfaction. In their view we are missing something because our lives are not closely knit with the lives of others around us.

Of course they are speaking from out of their own cultural context. They are comparing us to sociocentric cultures whose social ethic is based on mutuality. In his worldwide lecture tours Desmond Tutu introduced Western audiences to the idea of *ubuntu*. "My humanity is caught up, is inextricably bound up, in yours" he tells his audiences. "I am human because I belong. I participate, I share. A person with *ubuntu* is open and available to others, affirming of others, does not feel threatened that others are able and good, for he or she belongs in a greater whole."[5]

The idea of being good to others and sharing what we have is not original with Desmond Tutu. The world's religions as well as most traditional societies teach the value of good will toward others. The principle of the familiar Golden Rule is nearly universal. It promotes treating others as we wish to be treated.[6] Even in individualist cultures the rule is used to

3. Twenge, *Generation Me: Why Today's Young Americans Are More Confident, Assertive, Entitled—and more Miserable Than Ever Before*, 110–12 and 139–40.

4. Gardner et al., "'I' Value Freedom, but 'We' Value Relationships: Self-construal Priming Mirrors Cultural Differences in Judgment."

5. Tutu, *No Future Without Forgiveness*, 31.

6. Seligman, *Authentic Happiness*. Myers, *The Pursuit of Happiness*. Haidt, *The Happiness Hypothesis*.

encourage cooperation with neighbors. If I am good to others they will be good to me, and there are some things that we can do together that we cannot accomplish alone.

We hold back our enthusiasm when Tutu suggests "a person is a person through other persons." We are likely to accuse those who orient their lives that way of being codependent, symbiotic, or immature. Tutu's advice does not fit with our individualist belief that a person is a person by being true to self. Aspects of mutuality that go beyond a pragmatic understanding of the golden rule confuse us. The notion that doing good for others and receiving good from others are the same thing in the net effect of happiness does not fit our emotional math. For those of us raised to value freedom and self-sufficiency, mutuality is not unqualifiedly a good thing. What if others don't come through when it is my turn to be on the receiving end of the deal? Might it not be better then to rely on myself so I do not need to depend on anyone else?

Balancing self with not self, individuality with social identity, is a theme that captured the imagination of many cultural theorists in the early 20th century. The psychologist C. G. Jung suggested that in the modern era we have lost our "participation mystique" so that we no longer know who we are and cannot define ourselves by the past. We are "unhistorical," living in a rapidly changing present, and as a result we look for patterns of meaning by searching within instead of looking outside of ourselves.[7] What Jung suggests has become increasingly true in the United States as we have pursued our vision of personal freedom.

As we reflect on patterns that prevail in Boomer culture, it is clear that "you" and "I" understood as individuals are not "everyone." The "everyones" whose images we paint with broad brushstrokes as we attempt to describe a generation or an era are generic selves. The descriptions we give of them are summary impressions that function in our folk psychology. They are the guesses we make about what other people are like, and they are an effort to account for the pressures working on us that originate in the ethos around us.

If we pause long enough to listen, however, we also can hear the voices of those who resist these pressures. They encourage us to learn about the meaning of life by surveying how we have lived and seeing the consequences of our choices. Thoughtfulness, mindfulness, may help us delve more deeply into what it means to love our neighbors and do good, but it is not

7. Jung, *Modern Man in Search of a Soul*, 196–220.

likely that we can do this alone because the risk of falling back into the default of self-focus is very great. So the challenge remains, where can we ask the big questions? Where can we exercise the virtues, the ways of watching, that help us stay tuned to good? Where can we join with others to share the quest of deepening our understanding of these virtues?

IN SEARCH OF SPIRITUALITY

Current surveys in the United States reveal a complex belief structure behind an exterior of sectarian neutrality. Over 90 percent of Americans report that they believe in God or a higher power. Fifty percent report that they pray daily. Eighty percent say they believe in miracles. Some are active in the institutions of traditional religion. Others profess beliefs that once were taught by traditional religions but which they now hold privately in a modified way. In any case the statistics are a startling contrast to our snapshot images of generic Americans.

Consider for a moment the crowds in the stadium on Super Bowl Sunday or those who gather in Times Square on New Year's Eve. Are 90 percent of them Americans who believe in a higher power? Do 80 percent of the people in those crowds believe in miracles? Do 50 percent of them pray daily? There is no reason to think not.[8] What is surprising is how rarely we know this about individuals with whom we interact, unless we get to know them very well. Many Americans are "spiritual" persons who pretend they are not because they do not want to offend each other.

Some observers of this phenomenon have suggested that concern with religion in the United States is a lingering attachment to tradition, a residual set of habits that keep Americans connected to an Anglo-European past. There are many ways in which Americans have relinquished traditions. Why would this particular one be preserved? Unlike countries in which there is a state church or a sanctioned religion, the United States has expressly not allowed this.

Americans are religious by choice, and their religion is closely bound to their personal spirituality. They are free to give up their affiliations with religious institutions because no one requires it of them. By contrast when they persist in holding to these beliefs and practices, there is every reason to conclude that they do so because these forms of spirituality represent something significant to them.

8. Pew Forum on Religion and Public Life. "Statistics on Religion in America."

In our daily lives we are often spiritually anonymous. We cross paths with people as we go about everyday activities: riding the subway, waiting in the grocery line, paused before an outstretched hand at the toll booth, or ordering coffee from a barista who says, "Have a nice day." In these places we are generic, living only on the surface as anonymous persons. So few of those with whom we interact know what really matters to us. These are all manifestations of externality that contribute to spiritual loneliness.

For many shared spiritual practice is a means of overcoming the externality that frames much of their lives. Detachment and alienation motivate them to search for something to fill the void, and spirituality allows them to identify with something beyond themselves. It is their search for meaning. *A spiritual practice offers a way to enact respect for the sacred, and a spiritual community offers a place to explore what these convictions mean as a way of life.*

Despite the importance of religion to many Americans, its expression is often ridiculed in the public square. Perhaps that is why we have become more comfortable speaking of our spirituality and why we feel awkward talking about our religion. The term *spirituality* has the connotation of a more personal belief. Some sort of personal religion. Is the language we use, however, an accommodation that is evidence of spiritual shame? Is the word *spirituality* code for indicating that we do not intend to be imposing with what we believe? Is this a subtle way of indicating that we are not ganging up with others in a traditional religion, and thus we pose no danger or embarrassment to anyone else?

Though it is hard to explain precisely what the subtexts are, they hint at a certain collision of attitudes suggesting that we are free to believe as we do, but also that too much fervor in a community of belief may be threatening to others. Why do we feel forced to preface what we say with the proviso that what is important to us does not need to be important to others, and why do we feel compelled to reassure others that our beliefs do not pose a danger to them?

Our common life together is heavily influenced by the limits and allowances of the nation. In gatherings sponsored by the government or belonging to "the people," specifics of belief and practice are stripped away as much as possible. What remains is the most generic form of sacred tradition. Songs like *America the Beautiful* and *My Country 'Tis of Thee* are usually permissible despite their passing mention of God because it is the divine blessing of America they invoke. That is also why the President and members of Congress may end speeches by saying, "God bless you, and God bless the United States of America." Although some might object even to this, for most Americans the language is sufficiently nonspecific to be acceptable. We call this "being nonsectarian."

The freedom of the nonsectarian public square is accomplished at a high price, because, in our efforts to sustain a neutral *public spirituality* we purge our interactions with each other of much that founds our deepest convictions. We accept the spirituality of patriotism because it is that which we all are expected to hold as hallowed. What remains after we have purged our language and our practice of the specifics of faith is nobody's spirituality in particular. It is our common civic commitment without our personal foundations of meaning.

We claim that we neutralize the public square in order to protect individual freedoms; however, the same steps we take to protect our individual rights insulate us from each other. The expectation that good civic etiquette requires us to relate to each other only in terms of our common denominator of civic agreement also means that much of importance to us remains hidden. Who we are in the public square is not our most authentic self. It is a truncated self. Although we feel the obligation to restrain ourselves, we also want to believe that we are free to express ourselves. Is it freedom or the obligation to be socially correct that dominates public life?

I am not meaning to suggest that the common denominator of democracy has no value. Quite the contrary, the basic rights protected by the Constitution of the United States are intended to allow each of us to pursue our fullest good. Sometimes we do not like what others do with those freedoms, but we need only step outside the protections of this system and visit a country in which these rights are not honored to realize how important our basic freedoms are to us. It is quite possible to be critical of the way freedom is used without questioning at all the value of these basic principles of freedom.

Nowhere is both the protection of freedom and its abuse more apparent than in incidents like the judgment of the Supreme Court that free speech also protects Fred Phelps and his followers from Westboro Baptist Church who create brutal scenes at the funerals of veterans and public figures. It makes no difference that nearly everyone else finds this "hurtful speech" inhuman or repugnant. Phelps speaks freely, and that is the price we determine to pay to protect free expression for the rest of us. It is one of our most basic freedoms.

Despite the fact that we add our support to the importance of religious freedom, we forfeit too much if we fail to understand that there is more to our lives than what we are as individuals at the one extreme and citizens of a nation at the other. There is a vast field of experience between who we are as insular individuals, each with a name and a story, and who we are as one unit among three hundred million others, each identified by a unique social security number and protected by the same rights and freedoms. Between these two extremes, outside the hidden cloister of our individuality and in arenas far smaller than the nation, there is a middle space. It is in this middle space that we join with others to nurture our own particular religion or faith.

As government extends its influence more and more into this public space, rules for fair treatment by the government become rules for fair treatment in non-governmental associations. The demands of religious neutrality become pervasive until only in our most private spaces are we free to be religiously distinctive. At times the exposure of religion is simply not allowed, and at other times the social consequences for disregarding the pressures of religious etiquette (which means making our religion invisible) are great enough to stifle all but the most outspoken.

This is what happened when Archbishop James Conley of Denver met with a group of young Catholics at Stoney's Bar and Grill to share a beer and talk religion together. Some patrons began to harass them and some staff refused to serve them. Their offense was being too public with their religion. It made others uncomfortable.[9]

As a result of this confusion about religion we are isolated from each other in a very profound sense. We need others to help us define ourselves. We cannot do this in the culture at large, because when we try we lose ourselves. The currents of opinion are too big and too capricious, the scale of events too large. Furthermore, unless we are one of the select few who have a recognized public platform, we have no voice in the dialogues of mass culture. There is no real exchange that also includes us. We are observers whose voices have no audience, and we are actors whose influence has no impact.

How do we form our identities in the middle space? Do we absorb them from the company we keep? Is it gut instinct that lets us decide what feels best? Might it be that we pick patterns that maximize the benefits for

9. Gilbert, "Irony: Bar Boots Denver Bishop Giving Private Talk on Threats to Religious Liberty."

us? Or do we give shape to a common life through a group with which we identify? In a culture that defends individualism, each of us is free to do this as we choose, but the ways we do this make a significant difference both for us and for others. Freedom does not lift away our responsibility.[10]

It makes a difference if we live in a space in which selfishness is not reprehensible. We are easily confused if we are encouraged to live by our own rules and put ourselves first. It makes a difference if in our communal life morality is a side issue for which we show little regard as long as our behavior is legal. Unless we live in a shared space in which others hold us morally accountable, freedom can become an excuse to suspend respect for others and erode their dignity with our disrespect. Greed, often described as "getting what we deserve," can become the driving force in how we manage our finances, if we have no one to question us.

These examples and many others point to the value of living in a shared life space in which who we are and how we act is mirrored back to us. In the middle space we have the possibility of finding sanctuary for addressing life's big questions, and in that space we encounter others who challenge us to probe deeper by engaging in the search with us. For many Americans the middle spaces for carrying out their search for meaning are religious fellowships to which they bring their questions and in which they find others who share and honor this quest.

To understand ourselves we need to experience our place in a community in which we *actively* participate. A community is more than a set of ideas, and it is far more complex than a single project, or a website on which to post our opinions. In the life of a community we are visible. It is there that real events and shared experiences demonstrate for us the impact of our own choices. It is there that we are known by that which we value most deeply and that which has the power to steer our lives. In the shared sacred spaces of community we also clarify and elaborate those convictions that guide us, the moral standards by which we judge ourselves, and the deepest beliefs on which we anchor our trust that life is meaningful. The process is dynamic. In community faith lives and grows.

Contrary to the unappealing stereotypes with which traditional religions have been attacked by their most aggressive dissenters, it is within religious communities, not outside of them, that believers find both

---

10. Brewer, "The Social Self: On Being the Same and Different at the Same Time." Stapel and Koomen. "I, We, and the Effects of Others on Me: How Self-Construal Level Moderates Social Comparison Effects."

encouragement and freedom to open their minds and hearts as they search life's enduring questions. It is often within communities of conviction that old habits of injustice come to be challenged, that the new and surprising developments of modern life are encountered, and that the ongoing process of revision takes place. Despite their limits and imperfections, fellowships of faith offer opportunities to challenge and refine beliefs. That is a freedom we are not able to put into practice without the fellowship of others who stand with us in a shared vision.

All of this points to the problems created by insisting that the public square be religiously neutral and bland. Can we really know each other if what matters most to us is hidden? Can we really know the character of a man or a woman if what they value most is hidden from view for the sake of courtesy or not causing offense? Would it not be better to offend and be offended, and then learn to control those impulses in a way that creates exchange instead of conflict?

When we bring our spirituality out of the closet we become transparent, visible, and authentic. We do this by exercising the protections that liberty grants us to ally with those who share what we believe, and in these arenas we fill in the meaning of our freedom. We also do that when we step outside our communities of belief while being candid about the ways we are defined by them.

Some who seek the company of others to nourish their awareness of the sacred turn to new sources. Others who have come from long traditions of religion and spirituality take them up with new vigor as agents of change within them. And still others continue as they always have comfortably honoring the traditions of faith in which they were formed. The findings of the Pew Research Foundation suggest that about 25 percent of Americans leave the religious faith in which they were raised. This means, of course, that about 75 percent still identify, at least to some extent, with the traditions from which they have come.[11]

- Oprah was raised in the fellowship of a Christian church in which as a young child she was sometimes a speaker. As an adult she publically practices a faith that has no church, and she encourages others to take up the spiritual quest.

- Madonna was raised as a Catholic; as an adult she has turned to Kabbalism, a form of Jewish mysticism.

11. The Pew Forum on Religion and Public Life, "Statistics on Religion in America."

- Leonard Cohen was raised in a Jewish family, but he explored his spirituality through Scientology and Buddhism. In his most recent public statements he identifies again with Judaism, and its influence has been clear in his poetry and music.

- Pema Chödrön was raised as a Catholic but as an adult was ordained as a Buddhist nun. She continues to write, and thousands of people from all sorts of religious backgrounds attend her seminars and listen to her teachings on the Internet.

- Stephen Colbert was raised as a Catholic and continues to actively practice Catholicism despite the challenges he makes to all the religious traditions by television satires such as "This Week in God," which includes the irreverent "God machine" and a twist on religious news that pokes and prods religious sensitivities.[12]

We are a polymythic culture, although we struggle with what that means. As the battles about religion, spirituality, and diversity continue to be acted out in the public square, it becomes increasingly clear that the United States is not an a-mythic culture nor is it likely to become one. The flash points for disagreement change from time to time, and the lines of alliance shift. Times are changing, but there is little to suggest that our visions of truth and the convictions that guide our actions are converging on some neutral space.

Convictions, deeply held beliefs, worldviews that shape visions for action persist. In addition to the traditional religions that are easily identified, there are myths that are more distinctively modern. Some myths are philosophical, political, scientific, or humanistic. I suspect some myths may even be athletic if we take seriously the power of sports and entertainment to direct their followers' attention and define for them what is and is not important.

Not all secular myths use the language of religion, but their adherents pursue them with faith and devotion, nonetheless. Some secular myths are remarkable for their rage against traditional religion and for their confidence that science and rational humanism are necessary replacements.

---

12. Rohter, "On the Road, for Reasons Practical and Spiritual." Oprah, in *O*, the magazine that bears her name. Chödrön, *Taking the Leap*. Colbert, *I Am America*. Winston, "Stephen Colbert May Play Religion for Laughs, But His Thoughtful Catholicism Still Shows Through."

Listen to Bill Maher attack religion and observe how absolutely right he thinks he is.[13]

The variety of secular myths is vast. That is not surprising given that many of them are still in the process of invention. What seems to be absent from much of the public response to them is recognition that they too are religious, that they too are bound to a certain way of understanding the universe and what it means to live as a human in it.

Take as an example E. O. Wilson, a world famous biologist. He was raised as a Southern Baptist but left his tradition to become a secular humanist. His spirituality is centered on "biophilia," which is the love of all things living. The language Wilson uses to cultivate appreciation for biodiversity and preservation of the environment has the ring of religious fervor. It represents his ultimate commitment, a foundation of meaning that defines the course of his life. It too is a form of spirituality.

It appears that we are free to choose the foundation of our own beliefs, but we are not free to have none, unless of course we are willing also to sink into deep meaninglessness and succumb to random living, which ultimately leads to despair. Whether we actively choose the faith by which we live or accept by default worldviews that are formed around us, we have a context of belief. We cannot live without faith in something.

Those who are not active seekers often are taken up into the belief systems of those around them. Who has not heard the old saw that if you were raised by Christians you will likely be Christian, and if you were raised by Muslims you will likely follow Islam. Of course the old saw is simplistic given how often it is the case that children's views of religion and spirituality are quite different from those their parents would choose for them. It also neglects to see how much traditional religion adapts itself to new circumstances while maintaining its core convictions.

The influence of nurture on adults is not limited to religion, nor does a source of wisdom from a generation before make it necessarily unreliable. Furthermore, we might ask if being raised in a secular culture results in adults being secular, or if growing up in a consumerist culture will turn them into consumers. What is lacking in these broad jumps to quick conclusions about the effects of nurture is attention to the additional reality of real life challenges. To some extent our spiritual visions are also shaped by the real life questions we face, and these may change from time to time and from place to place.

13. Maher, *Religulous*.

If we determine to be intentional in forming our convictions, the questions we explore will be those that confront every generation, but also with every generation there will be a slightly different turn on them. They are not questions that can be answered intellectually and in one moment of decision. They are questions that are teased apart and worked through by living into experiences that challenge our conscience and unsettle our souls. They push us to honest reflection on the lives we have formed already, and they open our eyes to how our life choices impact our neighbors. These insights cannot help but turn us back to reflecting on where it is that we cast our own anchor.

In the middle of the twentieth century, just as the Baby Boomers were entering adulthood with a bold claim to freedom and just as their protests against the past were heating up, the philosopher and rabbi Emil Fackenheim warned that one of the responsibilities of freedom is to rethink and relive religious and moral truths. He wrote, "A truly free spiritual relation to the past is . . . the two-way relation of a genuine *encounter.*" The encounter he had in mind was not one between two persons but rather one between generations and eras. The encounter helps us to see who we are, and the comparison helps us to make judgments about who we believe we should be. It refreshes and brings to life again the most basic moral and religious questions.

What Emil Fackenheim is suggesting is that we are a lynchpin, but only briefly and for now, on which the past and the future turn. He goes on to explain that the encounter is "a relation in which the past, to be sure, is exposed to the judgment of the present, but in which the present also exposes itself to the judgment of the past. . . . Such receptivity, then, far from being incompatible with freedom, on the contrary enlarges and enhances it."[14]

Questioning the assumptions of their elders is one of the contributions that a younger generation can make to culture, but as the "forever young" generation of Boomers ages, they are finding it hard to admit their own religious convictions, and even more difficult to acknowledge their moral shortcomings. In the public square they submit to the narrow demands of political correctness that allow them to be outspoken about what they do *not* believe but rarely give them the space to admit what they do believe beyond the platitudes of freedom, prosperity, and happiness for everyone. How did we end up so confused about what is good, right, and meaningful?

14. Fackenheim, *Quest for Past and Future: Essays in Jewish Theology,* 140.

How in an age of freedom have we become so muzzled that we cannot speak about those things that matter most to us?

We all know persons who would have done well to question themselves. We all have known persons who loved themselves so much they never got around to being able to love anyone else. And we all have witnessed persons whose pursuit of their dreams did not pan out well. More important than what we see in others when we are critical is recognizing that *we* too have failed to question ourselves when it might have saved us from painful mistakes. *We* have failed to step up to the call of compassion. *We* have failed to do our part when taking the risk of caring might have advanced what is good and right. Some of our own dreams have turned into potholes on the journey. After living for some time we should be able to look back and see these things.

Our search for meaning, if we are earnest about it, sends us back to the sacred circles where, in the company of others, we clarify what we truly believe and determine how we intend to live. The process requires patience because what we discover about ourselves along the way may be uncomfortable, and the intentions we create for how we hope to live in the future may require discipline. This is where we disentangle from the hazards of mindless freedom. This is where we move beyond our reactions to the past and clarify a vision of the future tempered by the hard lessons of our own experience.

In honest fellowship we see the losses we ourselves have caused by the oversights of our generation. We see the spiritual vacuum created by underestimating the importance of belief. We also see how devaluing virtue obscured for a time the consequences of our lack of gratitude, our propensity for anger and hostility, our indifference about things we might have cared for, our recklessness about loyalty and enduring relationship, and our insistence that our lives should feel good and be painless regardless of what we do.

As we take the inventory of our generation we are faced with the many ways our embrace of random freedom fractured the commitments of the past and abandoned us to a deep spiritual loneliness. However, as we regain the company of those willing to honestly assess the experiment of our generation, we may still have the opportunity to discover a different sort of freedom that is grounded in spiritual conviction and shared in communities humble enough to learn from the past and courageous enough to dream the future.

14

A Last Chapter

*In a spiritually sensitive culture, then it might well be
that age is something to be admired.*

—Rowan Williams[1]

As I was getting ready to write the last chapter of this book I happened onto an article with the daunting title, "Why Last Chapters
Disappoint." The author suggests that many last chapters, some of them in
very good books, may as well not have been written.[2] The challenge of last
chapters also applies to the story of the Boomer generation. It is difficult
to find a closer for the story because the arc of the Boomer narrative is
far from complete. What is true of a generation is also true of individuals.
Though shaped by the decades through which they have lived already,
Boomers are in a transition stage for what is still to come. As they ready
themselves for growing old and are drawn to personal reflection, they
ask themselves about the meaning of life. The question does not feel as
abstract as it once did.

I considered, as a response to the dilemma of faltering last chapters,
not writing a last chapter at all, but that felt like leaving a visit without a
goodbye. It also meant that I would not have the opportunity to write about
some things that were still on my mind. What I wanted to communicate

1. Williams, "The Gifts Reserved for Age."
2. Greenberg. "Why Last Chapters Disappoint."

was neither a grand solution to the quandaries of the Boomer generation nor advice for younger generations so they can correct our mistakes. Both of these as last chapters would be certain to disappoint.

It occurred to me that I should explain why reviewing the events of my generation is important to me personally, and why I thought of putting my thoughts together in a book. This latter is quite simply stated. So let me begin with it.

I wanted to promote a conversation with other Boomers about our generation. Tossing out some old ideas and offering some new ones seemed a way to get the conversation started, a way to encourage readers to look at themselves and the stories of their own lives in fresh ways. I think about my own experiences of silent dialogue with authors of books. At times I put a book down for a few minutes and muse about what I have just read. Often I continue my side of a reading conversation when I repeat it to a friend over coffee because what I have read earlier is still tumbling around in my mind. Recently I borrowed a library book in whose margins an anonymous reader had penciled comments. They were tracings of a feisty response to the author, and as I read I was included in the domino effect of a serious reader's earnest concerns.

I like to think of this book as a conversation among friends. It ventures into topics that are already familiar to Boomers. It does not need to offer solutions or have a grand finale that wraps it all up because our lives will go on, and we will keep thinking about these things. Even if I had not been writing I would have been conversing about many of the matters discussed in this book. Writing expanded the circle of the conversation to include readers. And that brings me back to the other point. Book or no book, the story of our generation is important to individual Boomers, including me.

MILESTONES

Sixty marks an important milestone for many Baby Boomers. The worriers begin to fret about what could happen to them as they age. Take-charge persons review finances, pay attention to nutrition, and work out more. And those inclined to denial begin to tell jokes about old folks and pretend not to be one of them. Regardless of strategies for facing the years that are adding up, it is dawning on us that we are growing older.

Ask Boomers what they remember of the 1960s, and they get a far away look as they tell how much has changed. Ask them about the generation of their parents, and they admit they can hardly imagine what it was like to live in their era, surviving the Second World War and living within the confines of the 1950s. Few generations living now are as self-conscious about passing time as Boomers are. They don't let anniversaries of the big events of the 1960s pass unnoticed. The fortieth anniversary of the Summer of 1968 has already received ample attention, and the fiftieth will certainly be given its due. When Boomers look back at the 1960s they think of it as "our time."

Generation X, Generation Y, and the i-generation do not appear to have the same need to mark their own place in time. Perhaps they do not think of themselves as changing a culture or a nation. Maybe they see change as something that keeps happening. They are interested in stream- ing with it, but not claiming it as "their time." It is also possible that they are not reflecting on the past yet because they have not had enough an- niversaries to make that worthwhile. For whatever reason, the Boomers are at a stage of looking back at the events of their generation. That was Part I of the conversation of this book.

There are some things I do not want this book to be. I do not want it to be an "ain't it awful" jeremiad about the generations before the Boomers, as if outliving them gives us the last word. They were people like us living their lives in the circumstances of their time. Many of them are already gone, and those remaining are rapidly passing on. May they rest in peace, also in our memories.

Similarly I do not want to nag about the generations that are coming after the Boomers. We are not the pivot point of history. The legacy, which we are passing along, may create complications for those who follow us in time, and that is humbling. What they will do with these challenges I do not want to second-guess; in fact I want to trust them. They too will create a generation of circumstances, and they too will shape themselves as individuals in their time. Inheriting an imperfect world is the quandary of each generation. Like all others the newest generations will find their way, first energized by the spirit of youth and later sustained by the quieter reflections that come with aging. They, like us, will not be young forever, but for now they are.

AGE IS NOT WASTED ON THE OLD

My friends and I talk regularly about aging. We report to each other that we have aches and pains that we did not always have. Our eyesight is not perfect anymore. One of my acquaintances gave up skiing last year. Some of us move more gingerly than we used to when we walk across a slippery sidewalk. And sometimes we are surprised at the age of our own children. How can people as young as we are have children that old?

I call the bits of teatime conversation that I have with my friends our "sparks" of awareness. We are reminded in one way or another almost daily that we are growing older. The reminders are not the real concerns of aging, but like the little glimmers of a firefly they catch our attention for a moment, reminding us that time is passing. If we, either as a generation or personally, have unfinished business, then these sparks of awareness are telling us that it is time to get on with tending to it.

In a song that hit the top of the charts in 1969 Frank Sinatra sang: "I did it my way." When we were young and listening to Sinatra on the radio it was difficult to see the value of reflecting on the past. We could think of little worse than "doing it their way." We are not young anymore. We have accumulated decades of evidence that shows what life looks like *after* we live it our way.

It is not easy to grow old in a culture enchanted by youth. There are 70 million Baby Boomers in the United States, and there are approximately 55,000 people who have reached their hundredth birthday.[3] Despite all the evidences of aging around us, we are still a culture in love with youth. Some complain that youth is wasted on the young because we only value it as it slips away from us. Wasted youth might refer to the fact that we used to ignore wrinkle creams because our faces were smooth, and now we look cheerlessly at the ads that promise to remove lines and creases because we know our wrinkles are here to stay? Is there a more serious longing in our nostalgia about youth? Do we think our lives would be more valuable and our days more meaningful if we could be young again?

Several centuries ago in France the stage of life toward which Baby Boomers are moving was called "the age of decrepitude."[4] We are more careful now about how we refer to age, although our caution does not always cover up the disrespect about aging that is still deeply embedded in our culture. Organizations such as AARP (American Association for Retired Persons) publish information important to older adults and represent their interests to government and major corporations. The motto of AARP is "enhancing quality of life for all as we age." There are good political reasons for not ignoring us; we are a big group.

3. Haaga, "Just How Many Baby Boomers Are There?"
4. Thane, *A History of Old Age*, 199.

As Baby Boomers grow older being called "baby" feels dismissive. Perhaps that is why we more often now use the short form "Boomer." Compare the name of our generation to that of our parents, the Greatest Generation. Nothing babyish about that. Sometimes we call people in their sixties "senior citizens" or just "seniors." We call facilities in which older people live "retirement villages" or "senior citizen communities." They have nice names like "Sunset Meadows." When we were young it seemed fitting that we were called Baby Boomers, but now as we grow older we are stuck with a childish name. Personally, when all is said and done, I would rather be called "old" than "baby." Unfortunately "Old Boomer" sounds like an endearing name for my neighbor's dog. These reactions reveal our insecurity about aging, but they also suggest that we may benefit from viewing ourselves with a good dose of humor.

The Baby Boomers entering later adulthood during the first decades of the twenty-first century are pioneers in a new territory of expert aging. Innovations in medicine, social support systems, and new technology are being developed with them in mind. In 1935, when Social Security was established in the United States, the retirement age of sixty-five was set a few years beyond the average life expectancy of sixty-one. Most Americans assumed that they would work as long as they were physically able, and when unable to work any longer they would enter a brief stage of quiet retirement. Today the average life expectancy is edging toward eighty years, and many Americans anticipate that they will live long into retirement.[5] The time during which they will be described as "older Americans" will be a long life stage. What is this stage about?

As we grow older it is our turn now to look across the span of our lives. Although childhood is beautiful, we know more about life at sixty than we did at six. This should also make age beautiful. The expanding mind of an eight-year-old is a marvel. Just as remarkable is the wisdom of an eighty-year-old. That suggests that there is as much to prize about life at eighty as there is at eight. It is sad that so many of us give more attention to worries about whether we will develop Alzheimer's sometime in the future than we do to embracing the wisdom of age.

The brevity of life becomes more familiar as we grow older. Can we identify a purpose for living that goes beyond us and enfolds us? A purpose bigger than our own work and our own play, bigger than our own time and our own place? If aging is a time for consolidating what we have learned about life, then growing old is one of life's gifts. I was in the subway recently

5. Infoplease, "Life Expectancy."

and there was a poster that said, "It is a terrible thing to waste a mind."[6] The phrase kept running through my thoughts. Since then I find myself imagining a poster in the subway, which reads, "It is a terrible thing to waste age." Time is not wasted on the old.

THE TRIGGERING EVENT

Sometimes there is a wake-up call for growing older. It is a *triggering event* that may occur at retirement, the death of a spouse, a major illness, the loss of a friend, or a significant birthday that is a number with a zero. The realization of aging sinks in for some as younger people step into the places they used to occupy. We feel our years when we take note of the many ways in which our generation is no longer on the cutting edge of culture. The United States has elected a President who is too young to be counted among Boomers. Whatever the specific character of the triggering event, it drives home the realization that time is passing.

As we grow older we also experience that time ahead of us is growing shorter. Weeks fly by; months go quickly; years count off with surprising rapidity. We find ourselves saying, "Is it really New Year's Eve again?" or "It seems I just had a birthday and now here's another." The foreshortening of our future, however we imagine it, reminds us that we will not have forever to assemble our memories and gather our story.

Narrating our own stories uncovers the same questions that have been asked many times before by others: our parents, great figures in history, experts, and spiritual leaders. The fact that others have already grappled with profound human concerns does not exempt a new generation from living the same questions all over again. The human race may only have needed to discover the wheel, gunpowder, or penicillin once, but spiritual challenges come back to be discovered again with each generation. The triggering event reminds us that it is our turn to ask the questions.

BEYOND FREEDOM

If we live long enough to gain an overview of our lives, it is a gift. And it is an extension of that gift if we have years to reshape our lives so that they reflect what we have learned. The discernment that grows with time is different from a momentary opinion or a decision briefly considered. The

6. Billboards for UNCF (United Negro College Fund).

insights of experience are gained through being fearlessly honest about the long trends of our own personal lives. In the healing spaces of believing community where we rethink and reclaim commitment to moral action guided by spiritual convictions, we are invited to renew ourselves and understand others. And if we can muster the honesty, we may learn too to see the best and the worst in ourselves in the context of our generation and the culture it created.

The story of the Boomer generation is an unfinished story. So are the stories of Boomers' individual lives. We are beginning to understand that it is not within our ability to reroute history as we grow older. Will we grow old in peace and serenity? That, it seems, will depend on whether we can give up our search for the fountain of youth and turn our attention to the fountain of wisdom instead.

As we broaden our view and accept the humility of aging, we also begin to understand more profoundly that our story did not begin with us. We are only a small part of a much larger story, much larger also than the story of our generation. How we understand ourselves in the story of the ages defines us far more basically than any particular event of our generation or any particular moment of our personal life ever can. And our story does not end with us.

Placing our own story in the context of the story of the ages helps us break through our pride, set narcissism aside, and look honestly at our own behavior. It reveals to us our unfinished business. Whose lives did we alter by our disregard for consequences? Do we dare to make amends, recover broken relationships, ask to be forgiven for our own mistakes, and forgive those who have disappointed us? Of course, doing these things is no guarantee that someone else will change, nor will it perfect our lives. It may, however, untangle us from the tethers of ego and shift our perspective beyond freedom. It may turn our attention to wisdom, and wisdom is a good companion for the work of our aging years.

TIME FOR BLESSING

In time we will pass along many ventures that were important to us in the course of our lives. Our work. Raising children. Sharing communities. Planning the future. Being first in line with our opinions. Our confidence that we could be young forever cultivated a belief that we would always be in the center of things, that our convictions would always deserve to be the driving force. If we cannot relinquish this attachment to our own importance the passing of time will turn us into meddlesome, resentful old people. Or if all else fails and we weary of asserting our own importance, we may be reduced to indifference. Both prospects are grim. They are terrible contractions of life.

There is another option, but it depends on our ability to relinquish the future lovingly. We seldom do anymore what was done ritually by past generations. We make few occasions now for *offering our blessings* to those who will continue forward into a future beyond us. Sometimes we wish them "good luck" or give them gifts on special occasions, but rarely do we bless them.

We do not take seriously the worth of our blessings. When we were young ourselves we were not open to hearing the voices of the past; on the contrary, we ignored them. Their blessings were not what we thought we needed because we were working hard to disregard what they thought of us. Now we are in the odd position of being the older generation, and it is not surprising that we lack the confidence to assume that our blessings would matter much to those who are younger. They may not take them seriously, but that is not what matters because the act of blessing is still important to us. It is our turn to promise the generations that go after us that we will be their compassionate witnesses, surrounding them with love and good will.

There is another element in our blessing of the future generations. As we bless them we send them forward with the story of our own lives and the stories of others who we remember but who are no longer with us. When we honor our ancestors we carry their blessings forward, and when we bless the children of the generations following us, we also tell them something important about who they are. Offering our stories and our blessings bonds us to the future. We are the bearers of a continuing saga of generations. Understanding our connection to the past and our connection to the future broadens our own lives, and prepares us to embrace age with serenity.

RECLAIMING BELIEF

It takes a lifetime to question and sort our opinions. One of the gifts of age is clarity of vision. It is true enough that over time there are fewer things about which we dare to be dogmatically certain. Things we once thought plain and simple are less obvious to us as we grow older. Also what once we did not bother to consider may become more important to us now. Despite all the ways we change there are convictions that become more precious with time. These are things we know with certainty. There is comfort in naming them for ourselves. It is a profound test of our integrity.

Now is the time to gather up our courage and say, "This is what I believe." To do this is not to pretend that we can answer every question, but it is rather to declare openly where it is that we cast our anchor. By contrast skepticism, bred of fear that we cannot prove we are right, is hollow. Being intimidated by critics who threaten to discount us is wearying. Speaking our own truth compassionately is a great relief.

I like the quote from Søren Kierkegaard: "Life can only be understood backward, but it must be lived forward." Never has that seemed truer to me than in this stage of life in which the prospect of growing old seems to be moving nearer, and the invitation to reflect on the past seems more boldly inviting.

If the world changes in the future, and it most certainly will, it will be due to the efforts made by generations after us. Despite this our own last chapter need not be disappointing. We should not fear it. We are not the first generation to question what we were taught by our parents or to put to a test the religious teachings on which we were raised.

We also are not the first generation ever to face aging. As we grow into the years that complete our own individual stories will we be drawn back to the wisdom of the ages to sustain us in facing the limits and the mystery of life? We forged our freedoms, and now we are in a stage of life after freedom that requires more than freedom. If we can lovingly take our ground and accept the challenges of spiritual courage, it may be the most blessed.

> For age is opportunity no less
>   Than youth itself, though in another dress.
> And as the evening twilight fades away,
>   The sky is filled with stars, invisible by day.[7]

---

7. Longfellow. *Morituri Salutamus*, lines 282–85. These lines are the close of a long poem prepared for the fiftieth anniversary of his graduation from Bowdoin College in 1825. When he read it in 1875 he was 68 years old, and he lived seven more years. The poem honors teachers and those who had contributed to his life, and it honors the young who will continue on.

Bibliography

27 Club. http://en.wikipedia.org/wiki/27_Club.

Albert, Jan, Chad Mahood, and Amy Fast. "The Effect of Television News Valence on Arousal and Memory." *PSU Media Lab.* http://www.psu.edu/dept/medialab/research/negnews.html.

Allgor, Catherine. *A Perfect Union: Dolley Madison and the Creation of the American Nation.* New York: Holt, 2007.

American Journalism Review. *Walter Cronkite.* http://en.wikipedia.org/wiki/Walter_Cronkite.

Arendt, Hannah. *Eichmann in Jerusalem: A Report on the Banality of Evil.* New York: Penguin Classics, 2006.

———. *The Human Condition.* Chicago: University of Chicago Press, 1998.

Ariely, Dan. *Predictably Irrational.* New York: HarperCollins, 2008.

Asch, Solomon. "Opinions and Social Pressure." *Scientific American,* 1955: 31–35.

Augustine. "Augustine of Hippo—*Sermones,* 58." In *Bartlett's Familiar Quotations.* New York: Little Brown, 2002.

Baumeister, Roy, and John Tierney. *Willpower: Rediscovering the Greatest Human Strength.* New York: Penguin, 2011.

Baumeister, Roy, and Mark Leary. "The Need to Belong: Desire for Interpersonal Attachments as a Fundamental Human Motive." *Psychological Bulletin,* 1995: 497–529.

BBC. *Lab suspends DNA pioneer Watson.* October 19, 2007. http://news.bbc.co.uk/1/hi/sci/tech/7052416.stm.

Begley, Sharon. *Train Your Mind, Change Your Brain.* New York: Ballantine, 2007.

Bellah, Robert N. "Civil Religion in America." *Hartford Institute for Religion Research.* http://hirr.hartsem.edu/Bellah/articles_5.htm.

———. *Habits of the Heart: Individualism and Commitment in American Life.* New York: Harper, 1985.

Bellow, Saul. *Herzog.* New York: Viking, 1964.

Bem, Daryl, and David Funder. "Predicting More of the People More of the Time: Assessing the Personality of Situations." *Psychological Review,* 1978: 485–501.

Benjamin, Ludy B., and Jeffry A. Simpson. "The Power of the Situation." *American Psychologist,* January 2009: 12–19.

Berger, Peter. *The Sacred Canopy.* Garden City, NY: Doubleday, 1969.

Berger, Peter. "Western Individuality: Liberation and Loneliness." *Partisan Review,* 1985: 323–26.

Black Panther Party. "What Was the Black Panther Party?" *blackpanther.org.* http://www.blackpanther.org/legacynew.htm.

Bibliography

Blackburn, Simon. *Being Good.* New York: Oxford University Press, 2001.

Bloom, Allan. *The Closing of the American Mind: How Higher Education Has Failed Democracy and Impoverished the Souls of Today's Students.* New York: Simon and Schuster, 1987.

Boehm, Lisa Krissoff. *Making a Way Out of No Way: African American Women and the Second Great Migration.* Jackson: University of Mississippi Press, 2009.

Brewer, Marilynn. "The Social Self: On Being the Same and Different at the Same Time." *Personality and Social Psychology Bulletin,* 1991: 475–82.

Broad, William. "Orbiting Junk, Once a Nuisance, Is Now a Threat." *New York Times.* February 6, 2007. http://www.nytimes.com/2007/02/06/science/space/06orbit.html.

Brokaw, Tom. *The Greatest Generation.* New York: Random House, 1998.

Bruner, Jerome. *Acts of Meaning.* Cambridge, MA: Harvard University Press, 1990.

———. *Actual Minds, Possible Worlds.* Cambridge, MA : Harvard University Press, 1986.

Burger, Jerry. "Replicating Milgram: Would People Still Obey Today?" *American Psychologist,* January 2009: 1–11.

Bushman, Brad. "Catharsis Increases Rather Than Decreases Anger and Aggression, According to a New Study." *APA Online.* March 5, 1999. http://www.apa.org/releases/catharsis.html.

Capps, Frank J. and Thomas J. Curran, editors. *Immigrant Experience in America.* Boston: G. K. Hall, 1976.

Carson, Rachel. *The Sea Around Us.* New York: Oxford University Press, 2003.

———. *The Silent Spring.* New York: Houghton Mifflin (Mariner Books), 2002.

Casey, Damien. "Sacrifice, Piss Christ and Liberal Excess." *Arts and Opinion.* 2004. http://www.artsandopinion.com/2004_v3_n4/pisschrist-2.htm.

Chödrön, Pema. *Taking the Leap: Freeing Ourselves from Old Habits and Fear.* Boston: Shambhala, 2009.

Chase, Rick. "'Death of Hippie' March Ended Summer of Love in 1967." *Lost in the Sixties.* http://www.wcfcourier.com/blogs/lost.in.sixties/?p=23.

Clark, Geoffrey, and DeWitt Henry. "An Interiew with Richard Yates." *Ploughshares.* http://www.pshares.org/read/article-detail.cfm?intArticleID=9523.

Cohn, D'Vera, and Paul Taylor. "Baby Boomers Approach 65—Glumly." *Pew Research Center Publications.* http://pewresearch.org/pubs/1834/baby-boomers-old-age-downbeat-pessimism.

Colbert, Stephen. *I Am America (And So Can You!).* New York: Grand Central, 2007.

Cole, Michelle. "Bill Would Ban Smoking in Car in Which Children Are Passengers." *Oregonlive.com.* January 30, 2009. http://www.oregonlive.com/politics/index.ssf/2009/01/bill_would_ban_smoking_in_car.html.

Colvin, Geoff. *Talent is Overrated: What Really Separates World-Class Performers from Everybody Else.* New York: Penguin, 2008.

Confucius. *The Analects.* New York: Ballantine, 1999.

Cook, John W. *Morality and Cultural Differences.* New York: Oxford University Press, 1999.

Crawford, Christina. *Mommie Dearest.* New York: Morrow, 1978.

Creswell, Julie. "Even Funds That Lagged Paid Richly." *New York Times.* March 31, 2011. http://www.nytimes.com/2011/04/01/business/01hedge.html.

Crick, Francis. *What Mad Pursuit: A Personal View of Scientific Discovery.* New York: Basic, 1988.

Cronkite, Walter. *Eye on the World.* New York: Cowles, 1971.

Csikszentmihalyi, Mihaly. *Finding Flow.* New York: Basic, 1997.

———. *Flow.* New York: Harper, 1990.

da Cruz, Frank. "Columbia University 1968." *Columbia University.* April 1998. http://www.columbia.edu/acis/history/1968.

Dalai Lama. *An Open Heart: Practicing Compassion in Everyday Life.* New York: Back Bay, 2001.

———. *Ethics for a New Millennium.* New York: Penguin Putnam, 1999.

Davis, Kenneth C. "The Founding Immigrants." *New York Times.* July 3, 2007. http://www.nytimes.com/2007/07/03/opinion/03davis.html.

De Angelo, Rudy A. *The Cowboy Code.* http://members.tripod.com/rudydangelo/cowboy_codes.htm.

De Coster, Karen. "Henry Ford." *The LRC Blog.* November 23, 2005. http://www.lewrockwell.com/blog/lewrw/archives/009342.html.

Delgado, Jose. *Physical Control of the Mind: Toward a Psychocivilized Society.* New York: Irvington Publishers, 1971.

Dellinger, David. *From Yale to Jail: The Life Story of a Moral Dissenter.* New York: Simon & Schuster, 2001.

Department of Veterans Affiars. "Born of Controversy: the GI Bill of Rights." *Department of Veterans Affairs.* http://www.gibill.va.gov/GI_Bill_Info/history.htm.

Der Spiegel. "Laughing at Auschwitz." *Spiegel Online International.* September 21, 2007. http://www.spiegel.de/international/germany/0,1518,507175,00.html.

Dewey, John. *Freedom and Culture.* New York: Putnam's Sons, 1939.

DiGiuseppe, Raymond and Raymond Tafrate. *Understanding Anger Disorders.* New York: Oxford University Press, 2006.

Dodson, Eric. "The Post-modern Intensification of Humanistic Psychology: A Non-lecture of Disinformation." http://www.westga.edu/~psydept/dodson-nonlecture.html.

Donaldson, Charlie, and Randy Flood. *Stop Hurting the Woman You Love.* Center City: Hazelden, 2006.

Duran, Lauren and Beg Sulaiman. "Press Releases: 2007." *The National Center on Addiction and Substance Abuse at Columbia University.* May 7, 2007. http://www.casacolumbia.org/absolutenm/templates/PressReleases.aspx?articleid=487&zoneid=65.

Dutton, Donald G. *The Abusive Personality: Violence and Control in Intimate Relationships.* New York: Guilford, 1998.

Eagleton, Terry. *The Meaning of Life.* New York: Oxford University Press, 2008.

Edelstein, David. "Tony Soprano, the Hero As Villain." *CBS News.* June 3, 2007. http://www.cbsnews.com/stories/2007/06/03/sunday/main2878717.shtml.

Ekman, Paul, and Richard J. Davidson. *The Nature of Emotions.* New York: Oxford University Press, 1994.

Emmons, Robert A. *Thanks.* New York: Houghton Mifflin, 2007.

Epstein, Jason. "The Oscenity Business." *The Atlantic.* August, 1966. http://www.theatlantic.com/doc/196608/0bscenity-business/2.

Ericsson, K. Anders. "Expert Performance and Deliberate Practice." 2000. http://www.psy.fsu.edu/faculty/ericsson/ericsson.exp.perf.html.

Erikson, Erik. *Identity and the Life Cycle.* New York: Norton, 1959.

Evces, Mark, Dominic Parrott, and Amos Zeichner. "Effect of Trait Anger on Cognitive Processing of Emotional Stimuli." *Journal of General Psychology,* 2005: 67–80.

Fackenheim, Emil L. *Quest for Past and Future: Essays in Jewish Theology*. Bloomington & London: Indiana University Press, 1968.

Falkner, David. *The Last Hero: The Life of Mickey Mantle*. New York: Simon & Schuster, 1995.

Fantz, Ashley. "Noose Incidents: Foolish Pranks or Pure Hate?" *CNN*. 2007. http://www .cnn.com/2007/US/11/01/nooses/index.html.

Farber, David. *Chicago '68*. Chicago: University of Chicago Press, 1988.

Federal Communications Commission. *Golden Age of 1930's to 1950's*. http://www.fcc .gov/omd/history/tv/1930-1959.html.

Feldman, Elliot. "Frank Zappa vs. Tipper Gore." *associatedcontent.com*. August 22, 2007. http://www.associatedcontent.com/article/349977/frank_zappa_vs_tipper_gore .html?cat=33.

Felten, Eric. *Loyalty: The Vexing Virtue*. New York: Simon & Schuster, 2011.

Finder, Alan, Patrick D. Healy, and Kate Zernike. "President of Harvard Resigns, Ending Stormy 5-Year Tenure." *New York Times*. February 2, 2006. http://www.nytimes .com/2006/02/22/education/22harvard.html?pagewanted=all.

Friedan, Betty. *The Feminine Mystique*. New York: Norton, 2001.

Friedman, Howard and Leslie Martin. *The Longevity Project*. New York: Penguin, 2011, Kindle edition.

Fromm, Erich. *The Sane Society*. Greenwich: Fawcett, 1955.

Funder, D. C., J. H. Block, and J. Block. "Delay of Gratification; Some Longitudinal Personality Correlates." *Journal of Personality and Social Psychology*, 1983: 1198–1213.

Gabor, Andrea. *Einstein's Wife and Other Women of Genius*. New York: Viking, 1995.

Gardner, Wendi, Shira Gabriel, and Angela Y. Lee. "'I' Value Freedom, but 'We' Value Relationships: Self-construal Priming Mirrors Cultural Differences in Judgment." *Psychological Science*, 1999: 321–26.

Gasset, Jose Ortega y. *The Modern Theme*. New York: Harper, 1961.

Gates, Henry Louis. "The Root: Was Lincoln a Racist?" *Washington Post*. February 11, 2009. http://www.washingtonpost.com/wp-dyn/content/discussion/2009/02/09/ DI2009020901740.html.

Geertz, Clifford. *The Interpretation of Cultures*. New York: Basic, 1973.

Gergen, Kenneth. *The Saturated Self: Dilemmas of Identity in Contemporary Life*. New York: Basic, 1991.

Gergen, Kenneth, and Keith E. Davis. *The Social Construction of the Person*. New York: Springer, 1985.

Gerstle, Gary. *American Crucible: Race and Nation in the 20th Century*. Princeton: Princeton University Press, 2001.

Gibbs, Nancy. "Special Report: Thrift Nation." *Time*, April 27, 2009: 20–31.

Gibran, Khalil. *On Work*. http://www.katsandogz.com/onwork.html.

Gilbert, Kathleen. "Irony: Bar Boots Denver Bishop Giving Private Talks on Threats to Religious Liberty." *Life Site News*. March 2, 2011. http://www.lifesitenews.com/news/ irony-bar-boots-denver-bishop-giving-private-talk-on-threats-to-religious-l.

Gilot, Francois. *Life with Picasso*. New York: Anchor, 1984.

Gitlin, Todd. *The Sixties: Years of Hope, Days of Rage*. New York: Bantam, 1987.

Gladwell, Malcolm. *Outliers: The Story of Success*. New York: Little Brown, 2008.

Goleman, Daniel. *Destructive Emotions: How Can We Overcome Them?* New York: Bantam, 2003.

——. *Emotional Intelligence: Why It Can Matter More Than IQ.* New York: Bantam, 1995.

Gottfried, Martin. *Arthur Miller: His Life and Work.* Cambridge, MA: Da Capo, 2003.

Gottheil, Edward et al., editors. *Stress and Addiction.* New York: Brunner Mazel, 1987.

Greenberg, Cheryl Lynn. *Troubling the Waters: Black-Jewish Relations in the American Century.* Princeton: Princeton University Press, 2006.

Greenberg, David. "Why Last Chapters Disappoint." *New York Times.* March 18, 2011. http://www.nytimes.com/2011/03/20/books/review/why-last-chapters-disappoint-essay.html.

Greenspan, Alan. "I Was Wrong! Alan Greenspan." *YouTube.* http://www.youtube.com/watch?v=1bX_vhojH8c&feature=related.

——. *The Age of Turbulence: Adventures in a New World.* New York: Penguin, 2008.

Haaga, John. "Just How Many Baby Boomers Are There?" *PRB—Population Reference Bureau.* http://www.prb.org/articles/2002/justhowmanybabyboomersarethere.aspx.

Haidt, Jonathan. "The Emotional Dog and Its Rational Tail: A Social Intuitionist Approach to Moral Judgment." *Psychological Review,* 2001: 814–34.

——. *The Happiness Hypothesis: Finding Modern Truth in Ancient Wisdom.* New York: Basic, 2006.

Hardy, John D. and Timothy W. Smith. "Cynical Hostility and Vulnerability to Disease: Social Support, Life Stress, and Physiological Response to Conflict." *Health Psychology,* 1988: 447–59.

Harris, Gardiner. "Crackdown on Doctors Who Take Kickbacks." *New York Times.* March 3, 2009. http://www.nytimes.com/2009/03/04/health/policy/04doctors.html.

Hauser, Marc. *Moral Minds: How Nature Designed Our Universal Sense of Right and Wrong.* New York: HarperCollins, 2006.

Hayden, Tom. *Rebel: A Personal History of the 1960s.* Los Angeles: Red Hen, 2003.

Henig, Robin Marantz. "What Is It About 20-Somethings?" *New York Times.* August 2, 2010. http://www.nytimes.com/2010/08/02/magazine/22Adulthood-t.html.

Herman, Barbara. *Moral Literacy.* Cambridge, MA: Harvard University Press, 2007.

Hoffer, Eric. "Eric Hoffer Quotes." *Quotes.* http://www.quotes.net/quote/42643.

Hoffman, Abbie. *Revolution for the Hell of It.* New York: Dial, 1968.

Hogan, David. *The Sixties Chronicle.* Lincolnwood, IL: Legacy, 2004.

Hollyday, Joyce. "Grace Like a Balm." *Sojourners.* July-August, 1995. http://www.sojo.net/index.cfm?action=magazine.article&issue=soj9507&article=950752.

Howard, Michael. *The First World War.* New York: Oxford University Press, 2002.

Humphreys, Debra. "AACU Announces National Initiative on Fostering Personal and Social Responsibility in Today's College Students." *AACU.* June 21, 2006. http://www.aacu.org/press_room/press_releases/2006/CoreCommitmentsInitiative.cfm.

Iacoboni, Marco. *Mirroring People.* New York: Farrar, Strauss and Giroux, 2008.

InfoPlease. "Life Expectancy." *InfoPlease.* http://www.infoplease.com/ipa/A0005148.html.

Jamison, Andrew, and Ron Eyerman. *Seeds of the Sixties.* Los Angeles: University of California Press, 1994.

Janis, Irving. *Groupthink.* New York: Houghton Mifflin, 1982.

Joplin, Janis. "Me and Bobby McGee." *Janis Joplin's Greatest Hits.* Columbia, 1999.

Jung, Carl G. *Modern Man in Search of a Soul.* New York: Harcourt, Brace & World, 1933.

Kahneman, Daniel. *Thinking, Fast and Slow.* New York: Farrar, Straus and Giroux, 2011.

Kerbel, Matthew Robert and Matthew R. Kerbel. *If It Bleeds, It Leads: An Anatomy of Television News.* Boulder, CO: Westview, 2001.

Bibliography

Kessler, Jason. "Columbia Professors Get Images of Swatiskas, Noose in Mail." *CNN*. March 4, 2009. http://www.cnn.com/2009/CRIME/04/03/columbia.university.hate.mail/index.html.

Kingsolver, Barbara. *Small Wonder*. New York: HarperCollins, 2002.

Kosner, Barry and Ariela Keysar. "American Religious Identification Survey [ARIS 2008]." *Living in Liminality*. March, 2009. http://livinginliminality.files.wordpress.com/2009/03/aris_report_2008.pdf.

Kruglinski, Susan. "The Discover Interview: Marvin Minsky." *Discover Magazine*. January 12, 2007. http://discovermagazine.com/2007/jan/interview-minsky.

Kupperman, Joel. *Character*. New York: Oxford University Press, 1991.

Kurlansky, Mark. *1968:The Year That Rocked the World*. New York: Ballantine, 2004.

Lasch, Christopher. *The True and Only Heaven: Progress and its Critics*. New York: Norton, 1989.

Law, Lisa. "1960s Counterculture." *Arts and Music Pa.* http://www.artsandmusicpa.com/popculture/60'scountercult.htm.

Lepisto, Christine. "Shocking Space Debris Images." *Tree Hugger*. April 4, 2008. http://www.treehugger.com/files/2008/04/shocking-space-debris-images.php.

Liptak, Adam. "Justices Appear Open to Affirming Medal Law." *New York Times*. February 22, 2012. http://www.nytimes.com/2012/02/23/us/stolen-valor-act-argued-before-supreme-court.html.

Longfellow, Henry Wadsworth. "Morituri Salutamus." A Main Historical Society Website. http://www.hwlongfellow.org/poems_poem.php?pid=275.

MacDermot, Galt. "Aquarius." *Hair: The American Tribal Love-Rock Musical*. RCA, 1968.

MacIntyre, Alasdair. *After Virtue: A Study in Moral Theory*. Notre Dame: University of Notre Dame Press, 1981.

Mack, Annalou. "The History of Shockoe Bottom." *Helium.com*. http://www.helium.com/items/1371882-shockoe-bottom-in-richmond-virginia.

Maher, Bill. *Religulous*. Directed by Larry Charles. Performed by Bill Maher. 2008.

Maloney, Thomas N. "African American Migration to the North: New Evidence from the 1910s." *Access My Library*. January 1, 2002. http://www.accessmylibrary.com/coms2/summary_0286-5949581_ITM.

Mamas and the Papas. "If You Are Going To San Francisco (Be Sure to Wear Flowers in Your Hair)." 1967. http://www.lyricstime.com/mamas-and-the-papas-if-you-are-going-to-san-francisco-lyrics.html.

Marbley, Aretha Faye. "African-American Women's Feelings on Alienation from Third-wave Feminism." *Western Journal of Black Studies*. http://goliath.ecnext.com/coms2/gi_0199-6529501/African-American-women-s-feelings.html.

Marsh, Tim, and Earl Brooks. *The Complete Directory of Prime Time Network and Cable TV Shows 1946–Present*. New York: Ballantine, 2007.

Martin, Rene, David Watson, and Choi K. Wan. "A Three-factor Model of Trait Anger: Dimensions of Affect, Behavior, and Cognition." *Journal of Personality*, 2000: 869–97.

Maslow, Abraham. "A Theory of Human Motivation." *Psychological Review*, 1943: 370–96.

May, Rollo. *The Cry For Myth*. New York: Norton, 1991.

McCullough, Michael E., Robert A. Emmons, and Jo-Ann Tsang. "The Grateful Disposition: A Conceptual and Empirical Topography." *Journal of Personality and Social Psychology*, 2002: 112–27.

McCullough, Michael, Shelley Kirkpatrick, Robert Emmons, and David Larson. "Is Gratitude a Moral Affect?" *Psychological Bulletin*, 2001: 249–66.

McGee, Micki. *Self-Help Inc.: Makeover Culture in American Life.* New York: Oxford University Press, 2005.

Metcalfe, Janet and Walter Mischel. "A Hot/Cool-System Analysis of Delay of Gratification: Dynamics of Willpower." *Psychological Review,* 1999: 3–19.

Milgram, Stanley. *Obedience to Authority: An Experimental View.* New York: Harper and Row, 1974.

Miller, Randall M. *Ethnic Images in American Film and Television.* Philadelphia: The Balch Institute, 1978.

Moltz, James Clay. "Space Jam." *New York Times.* February 18, 2009. nttp://www.nytimes .com/2009/02/19/opinion/19moltz.html_r=1&th&emc=th.

Morgenson, Gretchen. "Report Criticizes High Pay at Fannie and Freddie." *New York Times.* March 31, 2011. http://www.nytimes.com/2011/04/01/business/01pay.html.

Muraven, Mark and Roy F. Baumeister. "Self-control and Depletion of Limited Resources: Does Self-control Resemble a Muscle?" *Psychological Bulletin,* 2000: 247–59.

Myers, David G. *The American Paradox: Spiritual Hunger in an Age of Plenty.* New Haven: Yale University Press, 2001.

———. *The Pursuit of Happiness: Discovering the Pathway to Fulfillment, Well-being, and Enduring Personal Joy.* New York: Harper, 1993.

Nagel, Thomas. *The View From Nowhere.* New York: Oxford University Press, 1986.

National Center for PTSD. "Anger and Trauma." *At Health.* http://www.athealth.com/ Consumer/disorders/angertrauma.html.

National Education Association. "Statistics: Gun Violence in Our Communities." *National Education Association Health Information Network.* http://www.neahin .org/programs/schoolsafety/gunsafety/statistics.htm.

Nielsen Media. "Television History." *Nielsen Media Research.* http://www.nielsenmedia .com/nc/portal/site/Public/menuitem.138fa1f1af8ff0919a69c71047a062a0/?vgnexto id=fb5579a21afc5010VgnVCM100000880a260aRCRD.

Nietzsche, Friedrich. *Thus Spake Zarathustra.* Cambridge: Cambridge University Press, 2006.

Nisbet, Robert. *Prejudices: A Philosophical Dictionary.* Cambridge, MA: Harvard University Press, 1982.

Now Public. "11 New Jersey Politicians Arrested." *NowPublic.* September 6, 2007. http:// www.nowpublic.com/breaking-11-new-jersey-politicians-arrested.

NPR (National Public Radio). "Havens Relives 'Freedom.'" *NPR.* October 3, 2007. http:// www.npr.org/templates/story/story.php?storyId=3845549.

Oakley, J. Ronald. *Baseball's Last Golden Age.* Jefferson: McFarland & Company, 1994.

Oprah. *O, The Oprah Magazine.* Hearst Magazines.

Pew Forum on Religion and Public Life. "Statistics on Religion in America." *Pew Forum.* http://religions.pewforum.org/reports.

Postman, Niel and Charles Weingartner. *Teaching As a Subversive Activity.* New York: Delta, 1971.

Potter-Efron, Patricia. *Anger, Alcoholism, and Addiction.* New York: W. W. Norton, 1992.

Putnam, Robert. *Bowling Alone: The Collapse and Revival of American Community.* New York: Simon and Schuster, 2000.

Random Acts of Kindness Foundation. *Practice Random Acts of Kindness; Bring More Peace, Love, and Compassion into the World.* San Francisco: Conari, 2007.

Rapping, Elayne. *The Looking Glass World of Nonfiction TV.* Boston: South End, 1987.

Rauchway, Eric. *The Great Depression and the New Deal.* New York: Oxford University Press, 2008.

Real, Terrence. *I Don't Want to Talk About It.* New York: Scribner, 1997.

Reilly, Edward J. *The 1960's: American Popular Culture Through History.* Westport, CT: Greenwood, 2003.

Rembar, Charles. "Oscenity—Forget It." *The Atlantic.* May, 1977. http://www.theatlantic .com/doc/197705/obscenity-law.

Riesman, David. *The Lonely Crowd.* New Haven: Yale University Press, 2001.

Rodriguez, Maddie. "Is Edwards Lying About Timeline of Affair?" *CBS News.* August 12, 2008. http://www.cbsnews.com/stories/2008/08/12/earlyshow/main4343941 .shtml.

Rohr, Richard. *Falling Upward: A Spirituality for the Two Halves of Life.* San Francisco: Jossey-Bass, 2011.

Rohter, Larry. "On the Road, for Reasons Practical and Spiritual." *New York Times.* February 25, 2009. http://www.nytimes.com/2009/02/25/arts/music/25cohe.html.

Rorty, Amelie, editor. *The Identities of Persons.* Berkeley: University of California Press, 1976.

Rose, Kenneth. *One Nation Underground.* New York: New York University Press, 2001.

Ross, Brian. "Edwards Admits to Extramarital Affair." *ABC News.* August 8, 2008. http:// abcnews.go.com/WNT/video?id=5544995.

Rudd, Mark. *Underground: My Life with the SDS and the Weathermen.* New York: Morrow, 2009.

Russert, Tim. *Big Russ and Me.* New York: Miramax, 2005.

———. "Excerpt from "Big Russ and Me"." *Dateline NBC.* http://www.msnbc.msn.com/ id/4926324.

———. *The Wisdom of Our Fathers: Lessons and Letters from Daughters and Sons.* New York: Random House, 2007.

Satir, Virginia. "Virginia Satir." *Think Exist.* http://thinkexist.com/quotes/virginia_satir/.

Savage, Jon. *England's Dreaming: Sex Pistols and Punk Rock.* London: Faber and Faber, 1991.

Scanlon, T. M. *What We Owe to Each Other.* Cambridge, MA: Harvard University Press, 1998.

Schachter-Shalomi, Zalman. *From Age-ing to Sage-ing: A Profound New Vision for Growing Older.* New York: Grand Central Publishing, 1997.

Schacter, Stanley and Jerome Singer. "Cognitive, Social and Physiological Determinants of Emotional State." *Psychological Review,* 1962: 379–99.

Schopenhauer, Arthur. *Counsels and Maxims (Kindle edition).* Prods. Josephine Pocolucci and Juliet Sutherland. Online Distributed Proofreading Team.

Seligman, Martin. *Authentic Happiness: Using the New Postive Psychology to Realize Your Potential for Lasting Fulfillment.* New York: Simon and Schuster, 2002.

Seligman, Martin et al. "Positive Psychology Progress." *American Psychologist,* 2005: 410–21.

Simon, Paul. "America." *Bookends.* 1968.

Skinner, B. F. *Beyond Freedom and Dignity.* New York: Knopf, 1971.

Smiley, Marion. *Moral Responsibility and the Boundaries of Community: Power and Accountability from a Pragmatic Point of View.* Chicago: University of Chicago Press, 1992.

Spielberger, Charles et. al. "Assessment of Anger: The State-Trait Anger Scale." In *Advances in Personality Assessment*, by James Butcher and Charles Spielberger, editors, 161–89. Hillsdale: Lawrence Erlbaum, 1983.

Stapel, Diederik A., and Willem Koomen. "I, We, and the Effects of Others on Me: How Self-construal Level Moderates Social Comparision Effects." *Journal of Personality and Social Psychology*, 2001: 766–81.

Steinbeck, John. *The Winter of Our Discontent*. New York: Viking, 1961.

Steinhorn, Leonard. *The Greater Generation: In Defense of the Baby Boom Legacy*. New York: St. Martin's, 2006.

Stephens, Mitchell. *History of Television*. http://www.nyu.edu/classes/stephens/History%20of%20Television%20page.htm.

———. "To Thine Own Selves Be True." August 23, 1992. http://www.nyu.edu/classes/stephens/Postmodern%20psych%20page.htm.

Supreme Court of the United States. "FCC v. Fox Television Stations." *Supreme Court of the United States*. April 28, 2009. http://www.supremecourtus.gov/opinions/08pdf/07-582.pdf.

Tavris, Carol and Elliot Aronson. *Mistakes Were Made (But Not by Me)*. New York: Harcourt, 2007.

Taylor, Charles. *A Secular Age*. Cambridge, MA: Harvard University Press, 2007.

———. "Responsibility for Self." In *The Identities of Persons*, edited by Amelie Rorty, 281–99. Berkeley: University of California Press, 1976.

———. *Sources of the Self: The Making of the Modern Identity*. Cambridge, MA: Harvard University Press, 1989.

———. *The Ethics of Authenticity*. Cambridge, MA: Harvard University Press, 1992.

Taylor, Stuart. "The University Has No Clothes." *National Journal*. February 11, 2008. http://nationaljournal.com/scripts/printpage.cgi?/taylor.htm.

Thane, Pat, editor. *A History of Old Age*. Los Angeles: The J. Paul Getty Museum, 2005.

Thomas, Marlo and Friends. *Free to Be . . . You and Me*. 1972.

Toffler, Alvin. *Future Shock*. New York: Bantam, 1984.

Turkle, Sherry. *Alone Together: Why We Expect More From Technology and Less From Each Other*. New York: Basic, 2011.

Tutu, Desmond. *No Future Without Forgiveness*. New York: Image, Doubleday, 1999.

Twain, Mark. *Christian Science*. New York: Harper, 1907.

Twenge, Jean. *Generation Me: Why Today's Young Americans Are More Confident, Assertive, Entitled—and More Miserable Than Ever Before*. New York: Simon & Schuster, 2006.

Ustinov, Peter. *Dear Me*. New York: Penguin, 1977.

Vonnegut, Mark. *Eden Express*. New York: Praeger, 1975.

Walters, Barbara. *Audition*. New York: Knopf, 2008.

West, Diana. *The Death of the Grown-Up: How America's Arrested Development Is Bringing Down Western Civilization*. New York: St. Martin's Press, 2007.

Westbrook, Robert B. *Why We Fought*. Washington, D.C.: Smithsonian Books, 2004.

Wilde, Oscar. *De Profundis*. Hertfordshire: Wordsworth Editions Limited, 1999.

Wilkowski, Benjamin M. and Michael D. Robinson. "Guarding Against Hostile Thoughts; Trait Anger and the Recruitment of Cognitive Control." *Emotion*, 2008: 578–83.

Willenz, Pam. "Violent Videogames Can Increase Aggression." *APA Online*. April 23, 2000. http://www.apa.org/releases/videogames.html.

Williams, Bernard. "Persons, Character, and Morality." In *The Identities of Persons*, edited by Amelie Rorty, 197–216. Berkeley: University of California Press, 1976.

Bibliography

Williams, Redford. *The Trusting Heart*. New York: Random House, 1989.

Williams, Rowan. "The Gifts Reserved for Age: Perceptions of the Elderly." *The Archbishop of Canterbury*. September 7, 2005. http://www.archbishopofcanterbury .org/articles.php/1518/archbishop-elderly-deserve-protection.

Wilson, Edward O. *Biophilia*. Cambridge, MA: Harvard University Press, 1986.

Winston, Kimberly. "Stephen Colbert May Play Religion for Laughs, But His Thoughtful Catholicism Still Shows Through." *Washington Post*. October 15, 2010. http://www .washingtonpost.com/wp-dyn/content/article/2010/10/15/AR2010101505758 .html.

Wyatt, Kristen. "Nooses May Be Added to Md. Hate Crime Law." *WTOP News*. January 16, 2008. nttp://www.wtopnews.com/index.php?nid=598&sid=1327798.

Yates, Richard. *Revolutionary Road*. Boston: Atlantic-Little, Brown, 1961.

Youman, Arthur and Roger Schulman. *How Sweet It Was*. New York: Bonanza, 1966.

Zacharias, Pat. "When Bomb Shelters Were All the Rage." *Detroit News*. April 1, 1999. http://apps.detnews.com/apps/history/index.php?id=48.

Zimbardo, Philip. *A Situationist Perspective on the Psychology of Evil: Understanding How Good People Are Transformed Into Perpetrators*. New York: Guildford, 2004.

Zoglin, Richard. "Rebel at the Mike." *Time*, July 7, 2008: 19.

CPSIA information can be obtained at www.ICGtesting.com
Printed in the USA
BVOW042042120712

295069BV00002B/1/P